The Reclaim Book

The Rec

Warming-up

contents

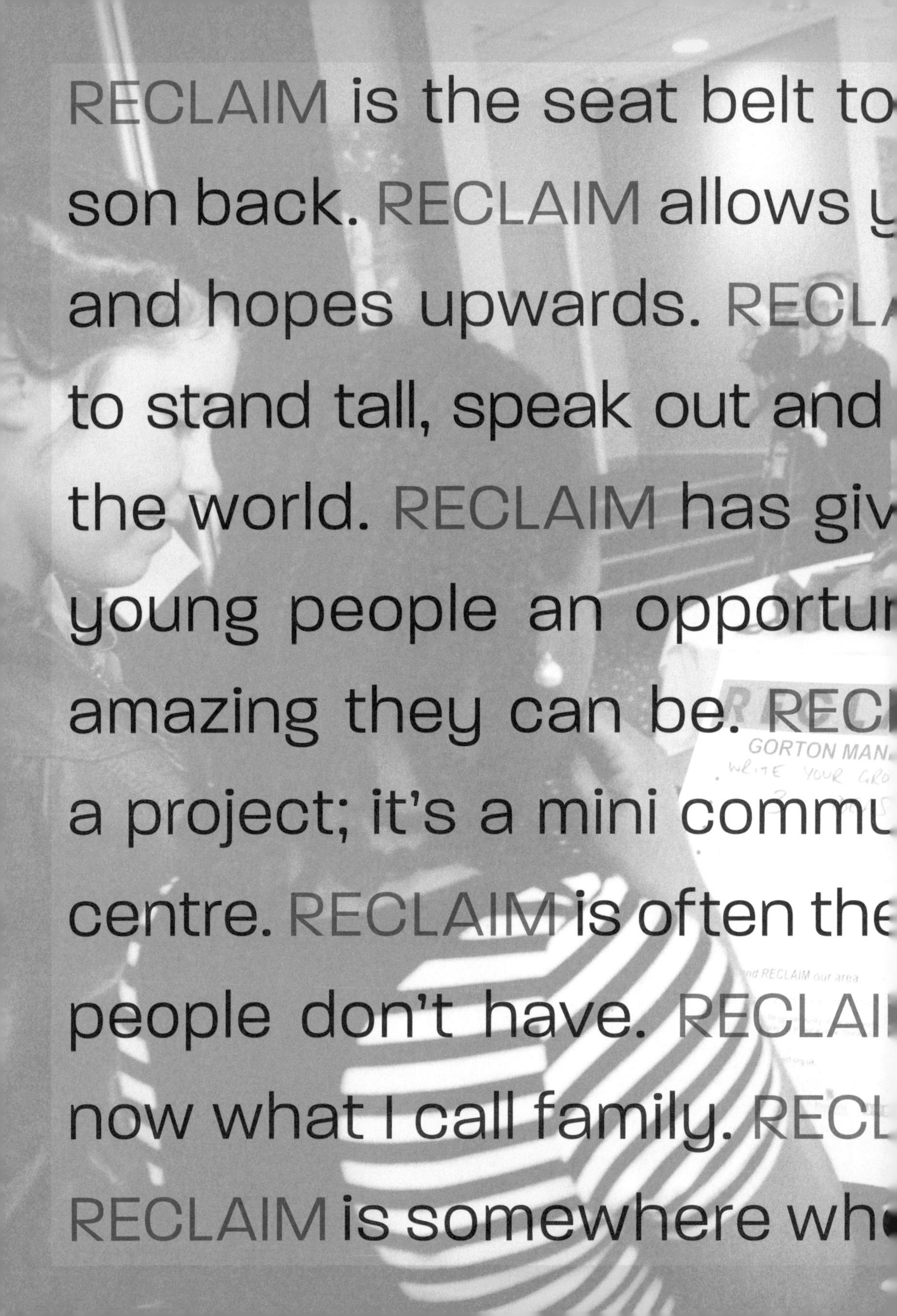

RECLAIM is the seat belt to

son back. RECLAIM allows y

and hopes upwards. RECLA

to stand tall, speak out and

the world. RECLAIM has giv

young people an opportur

amazing they can be. RECI

a project; it's a mini commu

centre. RECLAIM is often the

people don't have. RECLAI

now what I call family. RECL

RECLAIM is somewhere wh

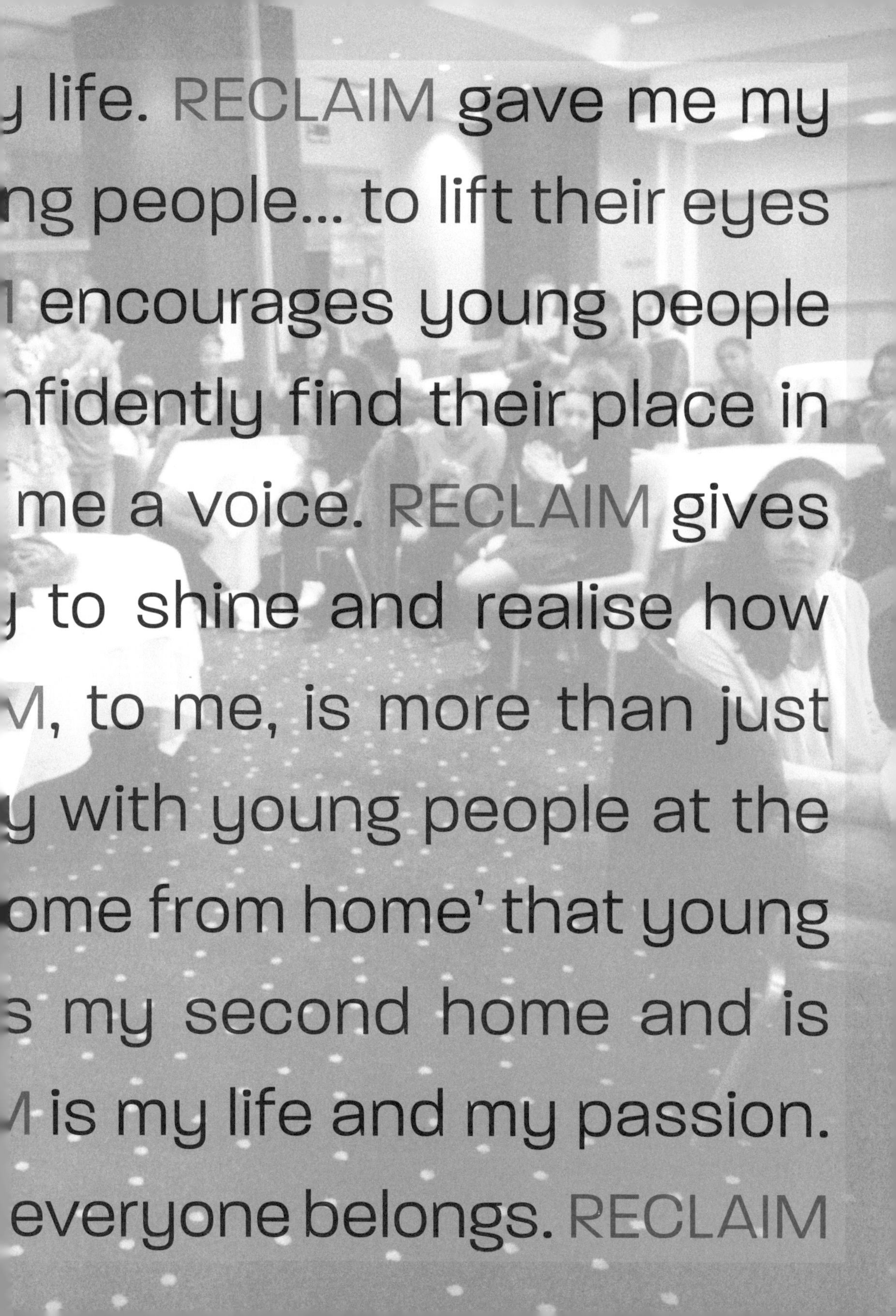

y life. RECLAIM gave me my

ng people... to lift their eyes

1 encourages young people

nfidently find their place in

me a voice. RECLAIM gives

y to shine and realise how

M, to me, is more than just

y with young people at the

ome from home' that young

s my second home and is

M is my life and my passion.

everyone belongs. RECLAIM

Manifesto Day for the Gorton Boys' Reclaim, November 2010.

Too Little Sunshine

There is not much sunshine in the working life of a journalist who writes mainly about prisons and the criminal justice system; not too many happy endings. Therefore, it was a welcome change and pleasure when I first visited and wrote about Reclaim in 2007. From the moment I stepped through the doors, I was overwhelmed by the enthusiasm and energy that flowed from all those involved in the project.

Usually, journalists write their stories up and then move on. In this case, I was so impressed by what Reclaim was doing, I have kept an eye on the organisation since and have been privileged to attend some of the conferences and graduation ceremonies and meet many of the young people who have taken part since that inaugural visit.

To witness the change in these youngsters, from when they sign up, usually shy and diffident (though going to great lengths to appear anything but!) to the confident, self-possessed graduates who emerge later, is to witness a transformation which endorses Reclaim's value more convincingly than words ever could. And it works every time; Reclaim does not rest on its laurels, it just gets on with changing lives and the atmosphere which greets each fresh 'batch' crackles with positivity and promise.

Adolescence is fraught with potential dangers, a minefield to be traversed with care. With one foot still rooted in childhood and the other striding towards maturity, young people are at their most vulnerable. Get it right and you have the makings of a good citizen; get it wrong and the consequences could reverberate through a lifetime.

I believe I can speak with some authority on the subject of getting it right, or wrong, with young people. Over half a century ago, growing up in Gorton, Manchester, I made a lot of wrong choices and, in 1957, ended up in a detention centre. The stated purpose of such institutions was to give young miscreants a 'short, sharp shock' and deter us from reoffending. It did not work and led, in my case, to an adulthood enmeshed in crime. And on subsequent prison sentences, I met virtually every member of the class of '57, proving the short, sharp shock did not work for them either. Of course we cannot change the past, but I wonder how things may have turned out for me if an organisation like Reclaim had been around to take me under its wing?

Now I write about the criminal justice system and preach against the folly enacted by politicians, of all persuasions, who punish young lives that have already been fractured by their upbringing. We lock up more of our young people than any other European country and the system fails them, and the rest of society, spectacularly; four out of five young offenders commit further crimes after leaving custody, custody which costs a minimum of £100,000 per year per inmate – three times the cost of sending a boy to Eton.

Contrast that with the aims and achievements of Reclaim. I visited the scheme again last year, through a comment piece in my paper where I compared Reclaim with other organisations involved in steering people away from danger. Many of these fail to deliver what it says on their tins, whereas Reclaim does precisely what its name pledges. But does it provide youngsters with positive leadership opportunities, and raise their self-esteem and aspirations? You bet it does. Likewise, Reclaim's commitment to encourage young people to challenge negative stereotypes of themselves and fight the demonization of young people in our society is to be commended.

On that last note; any literate alien perusing the media in this country would be forgiven for believing this generation of youngsters had sprouted horns at birth, such is the negative perception coming from so many channels. Phrases such as 'feral kids' and 'ASBO generation' abound, frightening many older people into believing that every kid wearing a hood is a threat to their personal safety. The fact is that kids today are no better, or worse, than the generations gone before. They may have different fashions, and certainly have different problems, but they are just kids and they need nurturing, not condemning.

This book follows the path of the Gorton Girls as they take the Reclaim road. Gorton has changed much since I grew up within its boundaries. Back then, there was certainly more material poverty than now, but employment was high and there seemed a general air of optimism; a belief perhaps, that better times were around the corner. But the factories closed and the area slid into decline.

What is depressingly evident now in Gorton — and other such troubled areas — is a different kind of deprivation, a marked poverty of expectation and aspiration, especially among the young. Constantly pilloried by politicians and others, intent on playing to the tabloid galleries, our children are conditioned into believing their postcode points them towards a limited future. But it need not be so; Reclaim allows young people from disadvantaged areas to lift their eyes and hopes upwards and gives them the guidance and tools needed to make the ascent.

Eric Allison
Prison correspondent, The Guardian

Why Reclaim?

Teenage life is hard. The stress is unrelenting: endless pressure to always look good; to excel academically; to be tested continually; to keep up with social media and to slot seamlessly into some pre-determined group. At home, some young people are also carers for younger siblings or for parents who are struggling to cope. Completing homework comes second to baby-sitting, cooking for the family or working under age to contribute to the household income.

The backdrop to these competing pressures is a media that so rarely profiles the positive actions of young people but instead prefers to focus on sensationalism. The unbalanced reporting of youth issues – such as teenage pregnancy and gang violence – has dominated this discourse and made it difficult for young people from neighbourhoods blighted by negative headlines to even have a chance. Manchester's Moss Side or Gorton will immediately conjure up impressions of 'feral youth' and lawlessness by those who have never visited and have little idea about the vitality and community spirit contained within.

We aim to find the young people in these neighbourhoods who face real barriers: crippling poverty, difficult home or school lives, low self-esteem or just general teenage angst, and work with them to offer credible and positive alternatives.

Reclaim is a simple concept that links young people from highly pressurised communities to a network of supportive and caring adults, proving that positive exchanges between adults and young people do still occur and not everyone believes that children should be seen and not heard.

We started life as an outreach project from Urbis, Manchester's centre of urban culture. The aim was to connect our architecturally-stunning and yet intimidating glass building with the communities that live only minutes away. We provided a prestigious centralised space to encourage young people to believe in themselves and to challenge the lazy stereotypes others held about them. Our first project linked 45 13-year-old boys from Moss Side with 27 adult males from their neighbourhood. For nine months these unpaid mentors ably demonstrated that their community was so much more than the lurid 'Gunchester' of tabloid headlines. What began as a small-scale effort to find fresh young leaders was immediately pigeonholed by some into a neat solution to 'black on black' gang violence. Significantly however, Reclaim was embraced by parents as vital support to keep their children on the straight and narrow and was cited by some participants as 'the seat belt to my life'.

At the beginning of every project each new cohort produces a Reclaim 'manifesto'. This document charts the hopes they have for themselves and all who live in their communities. The manifesto lists the basic tenets that will lead to happier, more cohesive neighbourhoods for all, in the words of the young people. What is admirable and shocking in equal measure is how much these public documents reveal about the difficult lives of many 13-year-old inner city children. 'Don't let killers get away with the crimes' was the first point on the first ever manifesto in 2007. 'Mums and dads need to act as one and become friends' from the girls in North Manchester two years later. 'No more drugs or drug dealing on our streets' was the call from Bolton boys who were exasperated and intimidated by the 'bagheads' in their town centre. 'Let us speak, we have a voice' clearly articulates the frustration that many of our young people feel.

Reclaim has grown and over 200 young people from across the Manchester area have been nominated by their communities and joined the process. The project has been successful with both girls and boys from diverse cultural backgrounds. Reclaim is always responsive to the specific needs of an area and relies on the young people and their communities to lead on identifying their priorities. Our small staff work tirelessly to support the young people; managing limited resources, constantly shifting political agendas and ever-dwindling budgets. The team is made up of committed, enthusiastic people from a range of backgrounds who work towards making a practical and positive impact with those who need it most. They are motivated by the young people themselves and the urgent need for non-draconian, effective intervention.

Having worked in both the state and private educational sectors, it is clear to me that the biggest barriers that exist for many of our young people are those linked to aspiration and access. You cannot aspire to something of which you have no knowledge. We have been privileged to meet fantastic teenagers who prove to us daily that with extra attention and encouragement, they are capable of great things. Reclaim aims to support our young people by showing them possible pathways and encouraging them to believe that with focus and dedication, most things are possible. Dream of life as a Premiership footballer, yes, but have a workable and achievable 'Plan B' in case Alex Ferguson never calls. To this end we run programmes designed to build self-esteem and confidence, but then outlets to practically employ these new skills such as job interviews, political and media literacy workshops or Fire Service training.

Over the years we have seen our young people develop into confident, impressive and talented citizens who will go on to have happy, fulfilled lives. Our hope is they will remember the support they received and volunteer to help support a young person in much the same way. Our young people are encouraged to stand tall, speak out and confidently find their place in the world. One boy chose the Reclaim motto that symbolises our project and underpins all that we aim to achieve: 'Judge the tree by the fruit it bears, not where the roots are laid'.

Ruth Ibegbuna, director, Reclaim
February 2011

Their lives are extremely complex. There's no routine or stability. When many of these young people get up in the morning they have no idea whether there will be food in the house, uniform to put on, or bus fare to get to school. Usually parents don't get up to see their children out of the house and, in a lot of cases, it's the child's responsibility to get themselves and their younger brothers or sisters out to school. If they don't do it, their parents won't push them.

Their home situation is often complicated. There are broken homes, private fostering agreements, large extended families with maybe older siblings, aunts, uncles or grandparents as the principal carer for the child.

Many of our pupils see school as a haven, a safe place, somewhere to be cared for and to be fed. Often the only proper meal the child will have that day is the one they'll get at school. It's also extremely common for children who have suffered cuts and bruises over the weekend – and once even a broken arm – to wait until Monday morning to get medical attention at school. They'd have no one at home who was able, or willing, to take them to hospital.

A significant proportion of our parents will not engage with school; some of them will have had bad school experiences themselves. They won't answer letters or come to parents' evenings. Some have 'given up' on their challenging child which is very difficult to deal with. In those situations you have to work even more closely with the child, helping them find a way to respond. In this type of school there are no formulae to follow; there is no right way.

Many children in these areas of benefit dependency don't understand why you would go to work. Maybe no one in their family has ever worked. They don't understand the concept of earning something rather than being entitled to it. It's not their fault – it's what goes on around them – but it is very worrying and we do our best to challenge that assumption.

We have had many successes and it's gratifying when pupils continue on to university or start a career but it's heartbreaking to know there are many more you have personally supported who have ended up long-term unemployed, or in prison, or as teenage parents.

Education shouldn't be just about English, maths and science. Yes, children have to leave school with qualifications that will equip them for the workplace, but if our aim is to turn out rounded citizens then we have to broaden children's horizons and help them see their place in the community.

Project work is invaluable. It's only when we take children on school trips that we realise the limit of their experiences. Some have never visited local art galleries or museums before and it's incredible to discover, as we do every year, that there are children who have never before seen the Town Hall. Whether it's school-based or externally provided, project work gives children experiences beyond the classroom, builds their confidence and helps them understand that they can make a difference.

I believe in our children. Given the same opportunities, they are as capable as all other children, whatever their background. Our children have the potential to succeed and, once they have, they need to be encouraged to bring that success back and help regenerate their neighbourhoods.

BUILDING A RECLAIM PROJECT

THIS IS JESS AND EMMA:

WE CHOOSE A RECLAIM AREA DEPENDING ON NEED AND WHAT FUNDING WE CAN GET...

... SOME COMES FROM TRUSTS AND BENEFACTORS...

THANK YOU!

...BUT IT'S HARD WORK GETTING THE MONEY IN.

THEN WE START TO RECRUIT THE YOUNG PEOPLE AND THEIR MENTORS...

... MOSTLY WE GO TO SCHOOLS...

YOU CAN NOMINATE SOMEONE FOR THIS EXCITING PROJECT

...THEY GET TO VOTE...

...AND TEACHERS HAVE A SAY TOO.

WANNA JOIN RECLAIM?

WE ALSO GO TO YOUTH OFFENDING TEAMS, PUPIL REFERRAL UNITS AND YOUTH GROUPS. WE'RE REALLY KEEN TO GET NOMINATIONS DIRECT FROM THE COMMUNITY: GRANDPARENTS HAVE A SAY AND...

...EVEN SHOPKEEPERS.

RECLAIM COULD HELP DANNY

WE'RE LOOKING FOR YOUNG PEOPLE WHO HAVE THE POTENTIAL TO BE YOUNG LEADERS. THEY MAY NOT YET REALISE THEY HAVE THOSE SKILLS... THEY MAY LACK SELF-ESTEEM... THEY MAY BULLY OTHER KIDS... OR GET BULLIED... THEY MIGHT BE VERY BRIGHT BUT DEAD SHY. IT'S IMPORTANT TO HAVE A WIDE RANGE OF YOUNG PEOPLE ON EACH PROJECT.

...VENUES NEED SORTING, FUNDERS UPDATED, SPEAKERS CONFIRMED AND PARENTS INFORMED. IT TAKES ABOUT THREE MONTHS BUT AT LAST WE'RE READY...PHEW!

EVERY RECLAIM PROJECT STARTS WITH A **FOUR DAY CONFERENCE**.

DAY ONE...

GOOD MORNING AND WELCOME!!

REMEMBER...YOU'LL ONLY GET OUT OF RECLAIM WHAT YOU'RE PREPARED TO PUT IN!

GREAT! FOUR DAYS OFF SCHOOL!!

WE KICK OFF WITH SOME 'GET TO KNOW YOU' GAMES.

THIS IS THE YES/NO GAME...

...STAND HERE IF YOUR ANSWER IS YES...

...AND HERE IF YOUR ANSWER IS NO

FOOTIE IS ALWAYS A GOOD ICE-BREAKER...

THAT DANNY IS A GOOD CENTRE MID

...NEXT THE YOUNG PEOPLE MEET THEIR MENTORS. THIS RELATIONSHIP IS CRUCIAL TO THE SUCCESS OF RECLAIM SO WE HAVE TO MATCH THEM CAREFULLY... THE FIRST MEETING CAN BE A BIT NERVE-WRACKING.

WHAT DID YOU SAY YOUR NAME WAS?

I'M MUSA AND I'M FROM GAMBIA

THEY THEN HEAR FROM INSPIRATIONAL SPEAKERS...

LET'S HEAR IT FOR EKE

LET ME TELL YOU ABOUT GROWING UP AS A BLACK BOY IN SOUTH LONDON

HE'S COOL

WHEN I WAS YOUR AGE, MAYBE A BIT YOUNGER, WE ALL PLAYED FOOTBALL THE WHOLE TIME. BUT WE'D SEE OLDER TEENAGERS GETTING INTO DRUGS, CRIME AND GANGS. WITH NO OTHER OPTIONS IT WOULD HAVE BEEN EASY - GLAMOROUS EVEN - TO GO DOWN THAT ROUTE. BUT I WAS LUCKY. I GOT INTO ATHLETICS AND FOCUSSED ON THAT. BY 18 I'D WON A PRESTIGIOUS INTERNATIONAL COMPETITION WHILE MY FRIENDS WERE GETTING INTO TROUBLE WITH THE LAW.

FIND SOMETHING YOU ENJOY - IT COULD BE ART, SPORT, EVEN COMPUTER GAMES - AND STAY FOCUSSED. IF YOU ARE DEDICATED YOU'LL MAKE A SUCCESS OF IT!!

... I'M A JOURNALIST WHICH MEANS I WRITE FOR A LIVING. I WRITE FOR A NATIONAL NEWSPAPER ABOUT THE CRIMINAL JUSTICE SYSTEM AND IN PARTICULAR I WRITE ABOUT PRISONS.

ONE OF THE REASONS I GOT THE JOB AS PRISON CORRESPONDENT WAS BECAUSE I'VE BEEN IN PRISON MYSELF. IN FACT, I'VE BEEN IN PRISON FOR 16 YEARS ALL TOLD, IN AND OUT FOR MOST OF MY LIFE.

WHEN I WAS A KID I WAS ALWAYS GETTING INTO TROUBLE. I DIDN'T LIKE SCHOOL AND SCHOOL DIDN'T LIKE ME. I STARTED STEALING AT A VERY EARLY AGE. I DON'T KNOW WHY I STARTED - THE REST OF MY FAMILY WEREN'T CRIMINALS - BUT IT CAME VERY NATURALLY TO ME. I WAS FIRST CAUGHT WHEN I WAS 11. I WENT TO COURT, WAS DISCHARGED, GOT INTO TROUBLE AGAIN, WENT BACK TO COURT AND BY THE AGE OF 14 FOUND MYSELF IN A DETENTION CENTRE.

PEOPLE KEPT TELLING ME I WAS *BAD, BAD, BAD*. AFTER A WHILE I STARTED BELIEVING THEM AND SO I CARRIED ON BEING BAD. I WAS LAST RELEASED IN 1999 AFTER A SEVEN YEAR SENTENCE FOR THEFT AND FRAUD...

I'M FED UP WITH HEARING HOW BAD YOUNG PEOPLE ARE. I DON'T WANT TO KNOW WHAT YOU'RE *BAD* AT... I WANT TO KNOW WHAT YOU'RE *GOOD* AT. THAT IS WHAT RECLAIM WILL DO FOR YOU. IT WILL FIND YOUR STRENGTHS AND BUILD ON THEM. IF YOU PUT YOUR HEART AND SOUL INTO THIS PROJECT THEN RECLAIM WILL PUT ITS HEART AND SOUL INTO YOU. I KNOW BECAUSE I'VE SEEN THE RESULTS.

CAN YOU ALL NOW WELCOME ERIC FROM THE GUARDIAN NEWSPAPER!

BEFORE THEY FINISH A BUSY FIRST DAY WE GIVE THEM SOME HOMEWORK: THEY HAVE TO WRITE A **PERSONAL MANTRA** AND BRING IT WITH THEM THE FOLLOWING DAY...

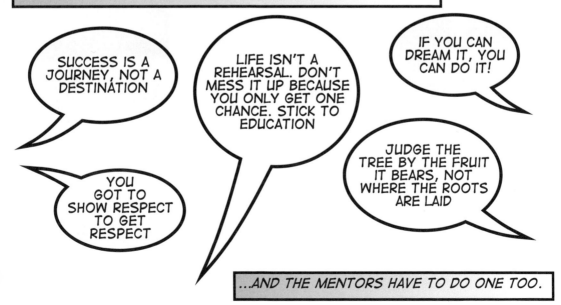

IT'S DAY TWO...

YEAH, YESTERDAY WAS BETTER THAN I'D EXPECTED

I'VE EVEN DONE MY 'HOMEWORK'

...AND TODAY IS **CREATIVE DAY** WHERE THE YOUNG PEOPLE SHOW OFF THEIR (SOMETIMES HIDDEN) TALENTS. THEY MAKE NEW FRIENDS, BUILD THEIR SELF-CONFIDENCE AND HAVE SOME FUN.

THERE'S SCRATCHING..

...T-SHIRT MAKING...

...RAPPING...

COME ON, I'LL START YOU OFF!

...AND ART WORKSHOPS.

I CAN DO THIS!

DAY THREE OF THE CONFERENCE IS **COMMUNITY DAY**... AND IT'S ALL ABOUT RECOGNISING THERE ARE OTHERS OUT THERE WHO ARE VULNERABLE AND NEED SUPPORT.

TODAY YOU'LL BE PLANNING SOME COMMUNITY PARTIES. YOU'LL GO SHOPPING FOR FOOD AND ACTIVITIES...

PARTY TIME!!

THEY ARE TRUSTED WITH THE MONEY...

WE'LL NEED PORK PIES, SALAD, HARIBOS, ICE CREAM, JELLY...

... AND HIT THE SHOPS.

YOU GUYS HEAD FOR THE SUPERMARKET AND WE'LL GET SOME GAMES...

SURELY THE ICE CREAM WILL MELT...

ANY DISCOUNT PLEASE?... IT'S FOR A GOOD CAUSE

SURE!

LATER...

THIS MUST BE THE PLACE

IT'S A LOT OF PRESSURE BUT THEY PULL EVERYTHING OUT OF THE BAG...AND GET TO WORK MAKING PARTY FOOD, PREPARING DRINKS AND ORGANISING GAMES...

IT'S DAY FOUR AND THAT MEANS **MANIFESTO DAY!!**

TODAY THE YOUNG PEOPLE WILL WRITE A MANIFESTO OF CHANGE FOR THEIR COMMUNITY. IT'S A PUBLIC DOCUMENT THAT THEY WILL DISTRIBUTE TO SHOPS, BUSINESSES AND HOMES IN THEIR OWN NEIGHBOURHOOD.

WHAT ABOUT: 'GET HIGH ON LIFE, NOT DRUGS'

GREAT IDEA! WELL DONE

I CAN'T THINK OF ANYTHING!

THEY DRAW UP A **SHORTLIST** OF THEIR BEST IDEAS... AND TRY HARD TO PERSUADE THE OTHERS TO VOTE FOR THEIR SUGGESTIONS.

THE TOP EIGHT IDEAS...

...ARE SENT TO THE **BBC** WHO KINDLY PRINT THEM AND WITHIN THE HOUR THE MANIFESTO IS DELIVERED BACK TO THE GROUP...

...60 MINS LATER...

IT'S HERE!

THERE'S SOME PRACTICE BEFORE THEY HIT THE STREETS...

'CUSE ME...WOULD YOU LIKE OUR MANIFESTO?

MANIFESTO? MANIFESTO? WHAT YOU TALKIN' 'BOUT MANIFESTO?!

AFTER THE CONFERENCE WE ORGANISE AT LEAST ONE GROUP EVENT EACH MONTH. SOME ARE CORE TO EVERY PROJECT, OTHERS DEPEND ON THE SPECIFIC NEEDS OF THE GROUP.
GETTING AWAY TO THE HILLS IS ALWAYS POPULAR...

BACK AT THE HOSTEL WE ENCOURAGE THEM TO MAKE MEALS FOR THE WHOLE GROUP INCLUDING THE STAFF AND MENTORS. SOME FIND IT EASIER THAN OTHERS...

EVERY RECLAIM HAS A COUPLE OF DAYS OF INTERVIEW EXPERIENCE. WE CALL IT RE:FOCUS AND IT'S LIKE SCHOOL... BUT HARDER! IT'S ABOUT RAISING ASPIRATIONS AND GETTING OUR YOUNG PEOPLE TO START THINKING ABOUT THEIR FUTURES.

ON THE FIRST DAY...

IT'S AN INTERVIEW WITH A *REAL* MANAGER IN A *TOP* COMPANY...

...THERE'S ADVICE...

YOU'RE ALL GOING TO WRITE A CV...

... AND ROLE-PLAY.

WHY SHOULD I GIVE YOU THE JOB?

ON DAY TWO EVERYONE GETS DRESSED UP...

THIS IS A NERVOUS SMILE...

...MINE TOO!

... AND IS SENT OFF FOR A HALF-HOUR INTERVIEW...

...AND FINALLY...

I DID IT!

AT THE LOCAL FIRE STATION...

...ANY BACK CHAT AND YOU'LL WALK...UNDERSTOOD?!

WHO DOES THIS GUY THINK HE IS?

WE FIND YOUNG PEOPLE HAVE SOME RESPECT FOR THE FIRE SERVICE AND SO WE ASK THE FORCE TO LAY ON A DAY OF FIREFIGHTING TRAINING. THE GIRLS GET TO DO IT AS WELL AS THE BOYS!

FASTER! FASTER!

YES SIR!!

THIS IS HARD WORK!

THIS IS A DAY ABOUT DISCIPLINE AND **RESPECT FOR AUTHORITY**. THE YOUNG PEOPLE ALSO TRY THEIR HAND AT SAVING A 'BABY' FROM A 'BURNING' BUILDING.

IT'S DARK IN HERE!

COME ON! EVERYONE WOULD BE DEAD BY NOW IF THIS WAS REAL!!

WHO'S GOT THE BABY?!

THE FIRE SERVICE HAVE AN AWARD-WINNING **BOXING GYM** TOO WHERE THE YOUNG PEOPLE AND THEIR MENTORS ARE TAUGHT HOW TO DEFEND THEMSELVES.

ONLY A FOOL USES HIS FISTS LOOSELY

TEAM-BUILDING EXERCISES ARE ESSENTIAL TO ENCOURAGE *COOPERATION* AND *TRUST*... THEY HAVE TO TALK TO EACH OTHER TOO!

HIGHER!

WHO'S TEAM LEADER HERE?

I'VE GOT HIM!!

HANG ON TO ME!

AS WELL AS THESE GROUP ACTIVITIES OUR COLLEAGUE, MELISSA, ALSO ORGANISES ONE-OFF PROJECTS TAILORED TO THE INTERESTS OF EACH YOUNG PERSON ON THE PROJECT...

GOOD AT DRAMA EH? FANCY MEETING AN ACTOR?

YOU CAN ALSO JOIN A SMALL GROUP DESIGNING A NEW YOUTH CENTRE IN YOUR AREA...

WE LAY ON THE LIMOS AND THE GOWNS...

...AND A POSH VENUE...

... SO PARENTS, HEADTEACHERS AND THE REST OF THEIR COMMUNITY CAN SEE JUST HOW MUCH THE YOUNG PEOPLE HAVE **ACHIEVED** ON THE PROJECT.

NOT EVERYONE GETS TO GO...IF THEY HAVEN'T SHOWN COMMITMENT, OR HAVE MISBEHAVED, THEN THEY DON'T BECOME **RECLAIM GRADUATES**.

THE GRADUATES HAVE A SAY...

I JUST WANT TO THANK...

...AND SO DO THEIR MENTORS...

...IT'S A **GREAT DAY** FOR THE YOUNG PEOPLE AND THEIR FAMILIES... AND IT'S A **GREAT DAY** FOR US AT RECLAIM. OVER THE MONTHS WE HAVE WATCHED THEM DEVELOP AND GROW AS YOUNG ADULTS AND WE KNOW OUR EFFORTS HAVE BEEN...

...LIFE-CHANGING!

I COULD GET USED TO THIS!

I FEEL SO PROUD OF HIM

IT'S ALL VERY EMOTIONAL

I HAVE MY SON BACK!

These are th

words and picture
by Len Grar

Gorton Girls

These are the Gorton Girls at Manchester City's stadium for the final day of their four-day conference, the very beginning of another Reclaim project. Thirteen-year-old Karla is having none of it. "I don't want my photo taken," she tells me emphatically.

On the first morning of the conference, Ruth Ibegbuna, Reclaim's director, stood in front of these 28 girls and told them straight. **"Anyone who thinks they're on a 'brat camp' should go home now. Just remember, you've all been nominated for this special project, you've all been hand-picked."** Four days on and the girls are buzzing. No one has been sent home. The mentors, volunteers and staff are exhausted and yet exhilarated, getting through today on adrenaline.

I know already the Gorton Girls have been busy this week. They've organised community parties at their local fire station and at a nearby primary school, experiencing what it's like to give something back; they've had fun composing their own raps and writing personal mantras; and they've been inspired by what they've heard from other young women. Recent 'graduates' Bonnie and Lucy have told them how Reclaim has changed their lives; Kemi and Tasha Ryan have described how, as young teenagers growing up in inner city Liverpool, they were manipulated and led into crime. The sisters, now reformed and employed as Reclaim outreach workers, encouraged the Gorton Girls to think for themselves and resist pressure from older troublemakers.

I know too that lasting friendships will already have been made not only between the young women but between the mentors themselves. **It's been a very special week so far and there is a charge in the room that suggests things are happening to these young people which, for some at least, will influence the rest of their lives.** "The young people we work with have to *get* Reclaim," I've been told, "they have to believe in it. If they are passionate about it, then it works."

"Okay, I'll shout a category and the first ones to run around and find everyone else in the same category are the winners. Okay, here we go: BIRTHDAY MONTHS!!"

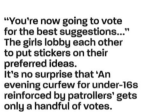

"You're now going to vote for the best suggestions..." The girls lobby each other to put stickers on their preferred ideas.
It's no surprise that 'An evening curfew for under-16s reinforced by patrollers' gets only a handful of votes.

"Quiet!" shouts Ruth. **"QUIET!"** The room gradually falls silent. **"This morning you have to come up with suggestions for the Gorton Girls' manifesto,"** she says. **"What would you like to make happen in your area? What could local people do to improve Gorton?"**

More facilities and activities for people of all ages to express themselves.

"We're not bad, we're bored!"

The manifesto is something of a Reclaim trademark, an 'official' public document from each project which, for the participants, sets the tone for the next few months. It's a wish list of aspirations.

Almost everyone gets down to work — but not Karla. She sits back in her chair, arms folded, determined to exclude herself. Gentle cajoling from her mentor comes to nothing.

"Think of it more as a set of guidelines rather than a list of rules," I hear one mentor suggest to the girls on her table. Ideas come quickly but this is a challenging task. **These young people are not used to being consulted and this is new territory. Here's an opportunity for them to say something about their area, their community.** These 'guidelines' will be printed as a flyer over lunchtime and within a few hours will be out there for everyone to see: Blu-Tacked to newsagents' windows; on the counter at the local library; at every café and health centre; stuffed in the leaflet dispenser at all the local schools and pinned to the notice board in the police station on Garratt Way.

The girls stand and read their suggestions out to the rest of the group. For most this is at least an embarrassment; for a few, it's torture. But there's encouragement from the mentors and the torture is soon replaced by relief that their turn is over and then satisfaction that they have completed this small but significant task. **The boundaries of their comfort zones are being ever so slightly redrawn.**

It's difficult to know whether this is the right house. There's no number on the gate or, as far as I can see, on the door. It's only the painted '3' on the wheelie bins in the front garden that gives me the reassurance to lift the letterbox flap and let it drop. The door is slightly open and I get a 'Come in!' from somewhere inside and hear the unmistakable clatter of advancing claws on a vinyl floor.

A small dog jumps up at me, barking, and then Karla's nana introduces herself and her grown-up son, Mark. "Would you like a drink?" she asks and, in the same breath, "Get down Tinkerbell!"

"I'll have a cup of tea please, quite milky. Thanks." Mark goes to the kitchen to brew up as Karla's nana shows me into the front room and settles herself in the corner of the sofa, her place. Pointing the remote at the large screen in the corner she turns down the telly as I position a tape recorder on the cushion next to her.

"Make one for Tinkerbell as well, would you Mark?" she shouts into the next room.

"She loves tea," she says to me. "Absolutely loves it."

"Where's her cup?" Mark calls from the kitchen and then, "Okay, got it."

"We can't give her coffee. She likes it but she goes off her head, a bit like a kid after too many cokes."

With the dog drinking tea from an over-sized cup at my feet, I try to get the interview on track. "I wanted to come during

"He wants to photograph us in the kitchen, Nana."
"In the kitchen? Why does he want to photograph us in the kitchen?"
"He says he likes all the ornaments and that."

the day, when all the kids were at school, so we could have a quiet chat. I'm a freelance photographer and writer and I've had a commission from Reclaim to make a book..."

"They've done wonders for our Karla," interrupts Karla's nana, "they really have. Karla has still not accepted our Bill dying. She's found it very hard to cope with."

I've come to hear about Karla's home life, to find out some background about this 13-year-old from Gorton who's found herself on the Gorton Girls' project. I've only been to one event and from what I've experienced so far she's not the easiest in a group of 20-odd young women all with their own challenges. She can sometimes be uncooperative, not working well in a group, and yet shows real commitment to the things that interest her. And now, with little encouragement, Karla's nana is telling me her story.

"Karla was only one or two when I took her in. Her and her four sisters. That was about twelve years ago. We'd had five of our own and all but the youngest, Michael, had left home when we took in Andrea's five kids. I was 53 and my Bill was 58 and even then he wasn't well. So I was looking after all those children and a disabled husband. It's been hard, very hard.

"Karla's mum and dad both drank. Andrea and Ged. He was the nicest fella you could wish to meet; he loved his kids. He went all over the country with his work, laying water pipes, and was only home at weekends. He was a real hard worker..."

"But he was an alcoholic?"

"Yeah, but a real grafter."

Karla's dad died of an alcohol-related illness when she was still a baby. "Andrea couldn't cope," says her nana. "She was pregnant with her youngest at the time. Ged's death really set her off on the rocky road. The kids would have all gone into care if she hadn't signed them over to me, and that was that. I've never *ever* had a social worker knock on my door."

I have to get this straight in my mind. "So, you and your husband had just about finished raising how many children?"

"We had five."

"And then five of your grandchildren move in?"

Karla's nana laughs. "Yeah. There was Yolanda, she was 16; Loretta must have been 10; Sonya was six; then Karla and Michaela, who was still a baby. At first the two youngest slept with us, Karla on a mattress on Bill's side and Michaela in a drawer on my side. That was before we'd got cots and that. Bill couldn't use the stairs so we slept in the downstairs parlour. The girls had the bedrooms upstairs.

"It didn't really bother me having them all here because I would have them all at weekends anyway. I'd pick them up from school on a Friday and drop them back on a Monday. The teacher used to say, 'We know they'll be in on a Monday at least,' because Andrea wasn't that good at getting them up and going. They missed an awful lot of school before they moved here.

"But no, I never had any help. I did it all on my own. The most help I got was off a charity called the Wood Street Mission. They gave me a cot for Karla and one for Michaela, and then a playpen, a highchair, clothes and toys. And after I'd finished with them, they got them all back. I still collect things for them now; my porch is full of stuff that I've gathered in. Every so often I'll give them a ring and they'll come and collect it. Last time they took 23 bin bags away.

"I haven't needed them for years, until last year when Bill died. Right from November until January I didn't have any money. After he died they stopped all my money and it took them that long to sort out my family tax credit. I got it all back eventually but I was living on my family, living on love. What else could I do but go and ask for some bits for the kids at Christmas? But they helped me out... ."

"They even sent you a care package, didn't they Mam?" says Mark.

"Karla has found her grandfather's death very hard to cope with. I don't think she's really got over it. They were very close.

"No, she absolutely loves going to Reclaim, it's done her a world of good. It's given her a goal. She seems more occupied, as if she's got something to focus on, when before she had nothing. She hasn't always got on well with school. The relationship has been a bit – what would you say? – a bit fiery at times. But now she seems to be getting her head down a bit more."

Gorton is just over three miles from the city centre but I've heard it described many times as Manchester's forgotten suburb. It's on the east side of the city and well known to some for its imposing, out-of-place, Gothic monastery and well known to others as the route out of town towards the Pennine hills. Some years ago the New East Manchester regeneration agency extended its boundaries and drew Gorton into its remit. Since then, new roads, a new indoor market and a massive rectangular Tesco superstore are the outward signs of progress.

In 2009 the neighbourhood marked its centenary of becoming a part of the City of Manchester. The 'Gorton 100' celebrations featured the return of a K1 railway engine from the city's science museum to the site of Beyer Peacock, where it was built 100 years ago by skilled engineers from a 2,500 strong workforce; a reminder of a proud, more prosperous past. But having touched the bottom, Gorton is now in gradual turnaround, and it has to be or there'll be little to celebrate for the next centenary.

During their pre-conference briefing, mentors hear that Gorton is a traditionally white, working-class area which, like so many other parts of British inner cities, has seen an influx of new immigrants, typically leading to tensions over housing and public services. The feedback from young people about their area is also familiar: no facilities, nothing to do.

This Sunday morning we are in the art classrooms of one of Gorton's two high schools, both recently rebuilt with all the latest facilities before the Government cash tap was turned off. It's an airy building with lots of natural light, but today it's eerily quiet without its 900 pupils. The plan this weekend has been for the Gorton Girls to work with the British Transport Police and make picture frames with multi-coloured mosaics that will be mounted on the platform fencing of a nearby railway station. Local primary schoolchildren have painted pictures to occupy the frames and the girls are adding colourful panels with their manifesto messages.

Nigel and Lorraine are here from the British Transport Police, grouting the mosaic frames made yesterday. It's already 10.30 and there are mentors, volunteers and staff from Reclaim but, apart from Karla, no girls.

It's a disappointing turnout and whilst Ruth is phoning young people, offering to drive around the neighbourhood to pick them up, Karla is concentrating hard with paint brush in hand.

This is her thing, it's what she is particularly good at and, before two or three other girls have arrived, she has already painted, 'Parents take responsibility for your children', and 'We're not bad, we're bored', with accompanying illustrations.

"She's really talented at art," confirms her mentor, Emily, when I interview her a little later in an adjacent art studio, "but she's always playing it down. She needs to be reminded of how good she is."

Emily hadn't intended to be a mentor. She was invited to speak to the young women on a previous project about how she'd turned her life around, making a bad situation into a good one. "I got pregnant halfway through my degree course," she tells me. "The baby's father's parting shot was: 'Enjoy your shitty, snotty, vomitty twenties!'. I spent the next nine months with a frown on my face but decided I wasn't going to be defeated by being a single mum. Instead, when my son was still a baby, I took him on my own to Australia – and went into massive debt doing it – just to prove I could. I went back to uni to complete my Masters and, four years ago, I started a blog – 'My Shitty Twenties' – which has won some writing awards and has now been taken on by a mainstream publisher. It's been hard but it's all worked out fine."

Since giving her inspirational speech, Emily has been hooked. **"I never thought I'd want to work with young people but Reclaim is very special. You'd think the young people would just go home and forget all about it but they respect what Reclaim is about. It works because they love it and are proud to be a part of it."**

And what of Karla? I know that on the Gorton Girls' project there was a change in the way the mentors and mentees were matched. Normally it happens on the first day but, as an experiment, it was decided to match them after the conference, once everyone had had a chance to get to know each other. "During the conference I could see how she felt intimidated by the other girls and often didn't want to join in with many of the tasks. She can be quite stubborn when she wants to be but, when I was at school, I was also different, got bullied and had an attitude so I could see quite a lot of myself in Karla. Apparently Karla said I was the one she trusted the most."

By lunchtime Karla's manifesto painting is complete, the mosaics are grouted and the group photo has been taken. The plan now is for the frames to be mounted on the platform fence in time for the 'grand opening' this afternoon when the schoolchildren, the Gorton Girls and the British Transport Police will be snapped by the local newspaper.

We've time to kill and the girls and mentors are taken to Subway next to the new Tesco. The assistant serving us is curious about who we are so someone puts her straight:

"We're on a youth project," she's told, "about building confidence and self-esteem."

After we've chosen between Honey Oat and Hearty Italian, between six-inch and footlong, and between Sweet Onion or BBQ Sauce, we

"Who do you think these secrets belong to?
I once had dreadlocks... my grandparents were opera singers... I once danced naked on MTV...
I own a goat... John Barnes was rude to me when I spoke to him on the street."

push tables together and start on our Meatball Marinaras and Veggie Patties. Karla catches sight of her nana disappearing around the corner of the sandwich shop and so she runs out to say hello.

At first our little gathering seems unremarkable. We've finished our subs and, as there is still time to kill before we're needed at the station, Abi, one of the Reclaim team, is organising a game of 'secrets'. We all take it turns to tell her something intriguing about ourselves that the rest of the group is unlikely to associate with us. "We've got some secrets," says one of the girls to me, "but we can't tell you those." Abi writes the secrets on a napkin and we all try and match the unlikely secret with its owner.

I look around the table at these young women, their mentors and volunteers. Then it hits me. The girls are enjoying quality time. It's what most girls their age would take for granted: a shopping trip with their mum maybe, a break for a sandwich and a chat, some one-to-one attention. Ours is a big family outing and these girls are put right at the centre by the adults around them. This day is for them. They are constantly encouraged, listened to and never put down. Not all of them are used to it.

Once everyone's secret is out we reposition the tables and head off to the station where parents have already gathered with their young children. The press photographer arrives, picks the cutest young boy and positions him with one of the Gorton Girls next to his picture of a caterpillar. I photograph Karla and Emily next to her manifesto painting. Karla smiles for the camera. "Look," she says, pointing to the council housing across the cutting, "you can see my house from here."

The next day I hear that the framed pictures and the painted manifesto had all been vandalised within hours of us leaving the station. Karla had watched it happen from her bedroom window and, incensed, she'd immediately phoned Reclaim.

By the time I next catch up with the Gorton Girls I have already missed a team-building activity in the Lake District, a creative weekend and a mystery challenge tour which took in the cultural hotspots of Manchester and Salford. But I'm here now – feeling out of place – for their pyjama party at a local community centre.

The large, multi-activity room still has its window shutters lowered which, with the bedside lamps someone has brought, helps to create the right atmosphere. This event has been the idea of Anna, an arts teacher and one of the mentors for the Gorton Girls' project. "Girls like to be in their pyjamas," she tells me as they begin to arrive, "hanging around with their friends. That's when the real talking happens and you find out about each other and share problems." **But, this being Reclaim, it's a pyjama party with a difference. After the hot chocolates have been finished, the marker pens and paper come out and the girls get down to work.**

The group is told that in a couple of weeks they will be taking time off school to do some interview training. Something to prepare them for the world of work. This afternoon they are going to have a brainstorm about their own personal qualities and what they think they can offer an employer.

They split into four groups, spread themselves around the room, and work on different tasks.

"What qualities do you think employers are looking for?" asks Anna whose group is trying to decide what makes a good CV.

"You've got to be punctual," says one girl.

"Good, and what do you need to get from school that will make your CV look amazing?"

"You've got to get your GCSEs, specially English and maths," say the girls.

"Good, get it down," says Anna.

"I want to be an actress," says Alix. "Do I still need those?"

"Oh yes, you've still got to have them... and what other qualifications do you think you'd need?"

Alix is one of the girls I've been asked to profile for this book and, although my first impressions are of a confident young woman who doesn't have a care in the world, I've been told she's been suffering some serious bullying which she's found difficult to deal with. There's some turmoil under that easy smile.

Meanwhile Karla has wrapped herself in the large leopard-pattern blanket she has brought from home, hiding herself underneath whenever it suits. "Come on, Karla, you really need to join in this bit," encourages Emily. Karla and her small group write a list of questions that might get asked in an interview and although she's not that forthcoming in making suggestions she is right up there when it comes to presenting their findings to the rest of the group.

Alix heads her trio when it comes to their turn to explain what will make a good CV.

"They might ask you things like:
'What are you good at? What are your hobbies? Do you have good leadership skills?
What did you do for work experience?'"

What event do you think would encourage everyone to come

After all the teams have presented their ideas there's a break for more hot chocolate and an impromptu Haribo-eating contest, the photos from which I promise not to publish.

Although all the girls here have really got stuck into the task and had a good laugh in the process, the Reclaim staff are still disappointed that only a small number of girls have, yet again, shown up. So, once mouths are again empty, they bring everyone together for a bit of a brainstorm. "What event do you think would encourage everyone to come together at a weekend?" asks Ruth.

"I think more people would come if we did something about hair and beauty. Maybe they could make up their mentors," one of the volunteers suggests.

"Make-over your mentor! Now that's an event," enthuses Ruth. "Love it!" There's a round of applause. The girls love it too.

"So what about this?" says Ruth, cogs whirring. "We give each mentee some money, ten pounds or whatever, and you have to go down to the charity shops in town and work with your mentor to make them look great. I think that could really work!"

"What do you think of that, Karla?" asks Emily. "And you can be as cruel as you like." Karla likes the idea.

Helen and Alix throw themselves into the task with Alix demonstrating her acting capabilities. "Alix is kind, friendly, inventive, smiley, enthusiastic and silly... and she is a dolphin!"

The afternoon continues with the girls invited to think about their positive qualities as a warm-up to the upcoming interview workshop where they will have to write their own CVs. They pair off, some with mentors and some with other girls and write down each other's good points. It's a fun, confidence-boosting exercise which becomes hilarious when it's announced that everyone now has to come up with the name of an animal that shares the same characteristics as their own... and they have to impersonate that animal in front of the group!

One girl is described by her partner as: friendly, pretty, brave, stylish and chatty — which makes her a shire horse. There's also a cat, a flamingo, a dragon and an Andrex puppy. Bouncing across the room, whooping, Anna does a fine representation of a spider monkey before

Karla and Emily come forward, Karla sitting on the floor with only her head peeking out of her oversize blanket.

"Karla says I have to read out both of ours, so mine first," says Emily with Karla at her feet. "I am, apparently: unique, fantastic, wonderful, arty and good at drawing and therefore I am a parrot."

With a last minute surge of confidence Karla takes the paper from Emily and reads:

"I am clever and funny, shy, good at swimming, soft on the inside, so I am a sea turtle... and this is my shell," she says as she again draws the blanket around herself.

There's cheering and clapping as the final animals reveal themselves. "Well done," says Ruth. "Well done! That was a really nice group of creatures. Now, have we got time to do some face-painting?"

A few days later I call Alix's mum to make an arrangement to interview her. "Oh yes, Alix has told me all about you," Anita says. "She's going in a book, isn't she?"

Alix lives in east Manchester with her twin sister and her mum and dad. Technically she's not a Gorton girl but the Catholic secondary school she attends just about squeezes into Gorton's boundaries which is why she's in. Both her parents work at the city's main hospital, her mum as a nurse and her dad as a porter. She has two older half-sisters from her dad's previous marriage.

We've arranged for a chat on one of Anita's days off. She's having a lazy day, still in her slippers when I arrive at their pristine home tucked in the side of a cul-de-sac.

"What's in there?" I ask, as I put my bags down next to an empty fish tank with one of those lights across the top, like a snooker table. "Oh, don't worry," says Anita, "it's just a corn snake."

After setting up my tape recorders and, with mug in hand, I ask Anita to start at the beginning.

"It was our second attempt at IVF when I conceived with the girls," she begins, "the first time it didn't work and then we had to wait a year before we could try again but then it worked. We actually saw the egg dividing under the microscope before they put it back inside me, which was really weird."

"How exciting was that?"

At first I position them all on the sofa but Dave blinks on nearly every one of my 20 or so shots. It's as if he knows exactly when the flash will go off. Incredible. We go outside in the fading light for another attempt.

"Yeah, that was really good, very exciting. I was so determined it was going to work that, when I got home from the hospital, I stayed in bed for a fortnight with my feet up on the wall.

"I was in a lot of pain during the pregnancy and I was taken in for a caesarean two weeks early and then my girls came along. I don't know where the names Alix and Mia came from, we just wanted something different. I chose Mia and Dave chose Alix, but with an 'i' instead of an 'e'. I don't know why."

"Who is the eldest?"

"Alix, by one minute, and she will never, ever, let Mia forget it. But they've always been very close, ever since they were little babies. They used to have their own cots and I'd put them side by side and their hands used to go through the bars and they'd be holding hands with each other.

"By the time they'd started primary school they'd both developed their own personalities. Mia had become more boyish – more tomboy really – and Alix was very 'girly girly', but there was still a closeness that you wouldn't believe and they'd always stick up for each other. Mia is very laid back, too laid back really, and Alix is very sensitive: she takes everything on board, whereas Mia takes it all with a pinch of salt."

I ask about school. Alix, I am told, is in the top set and Mia is in the bottom. "Mia's not mithered whereas Alix wants to do really well. I'm trying to get Mia excited about things."

And what about Reclaim? Why, I wonder is only Alix on the Gorton Girls' project? "Oh, they both came home full of it, both wanted to do it. But Mia's teacher wouldn't let her out of the classroom and, by the time she'd made it to the room where they were signing up, it was too late. She was extremely upset and it took her a long time to get over it. But now she's really happy that her sister is doing it and every time Alix goes to Reclaim, we take Mia out for a treat.

"She's loving it, really loving it. She's made a couple of good friends and that's good for Alix because ever since the end of primary she's been bullied, and still is."

Anita tells me about the source of the bullying, some of the experiences Alix has endured, the counselling that didn't really work."

"So friendships are important to Alix, she really treasures them. Since Reclaim she's been able to handle things a lot better, it's helped her realise that what's gone on in the past isn't her doing. So yes, Reclaim has been good for her."

"In this country people don't like to show off but in a CV you really have to sell yourself. In Nigeria we think we are great and we tell everyone we are great whether they want to hear it or not. So, in the next 30 seconds think of one thing you are brilliant at... and think like a Nigerian!"

"It's in these two days that the young people realise what Reclaim is all about. The penny drops," says Ruth as we wait for the coach to arrive. We are in the exhibition space of an inner city arts centre which, nearly 100 years ago, was established as the Zion Institute with a mission 'for local people to renew their body, mind and soul'. And so the work goes on.

It's a school day and so attendance amongst the girls is high: this is better than their regular lessons. But because it's during the week not many of the mentors can take time off to attend. This is a dilemma for Reclaim and one that's probably unreconcilable. Weekday events are great for the mentees whereas mentors are more likely to be available at weekends. Many of the working mentors take annual leave to attend the four-day conference at the beginning of the project but are understandably reluctant to use too much of their holiday entitlement for Reclaim. Despite the small mentor numbers there are plenty of Reclaim staff and volunteers and each table of girls has at least one adult to help with the tasks ahead.

"Tomorrow you're going for a job interview," says Ruth as the 20 or so young people settle themselves down in pre-determined groups. **"Some of you don't think this is going to happen, but it is. We've been working with different organisations around town, like the NHS and the British Transport Police. Their managers will receive copies**

of your CVs later and tomorrow you will have a half-hour interview with one of them." There's a look of incredulity on the girls' faces.

"So," shouts Ruth above the stunned silence. "Who knows what a CV is?"

Towards the back of the room Paige's hand goes up and she gives an almost dictionary definition. "That's absolutely brilliant," encourages Ruth. "For those of you who didn't hear that: a CV is where you put down all your experiences, your qualifications, what your skills are..."

"Can you make it up?" someone interrupts.

"No, you cannot make it up."

"I mean, for tomorrow. Can you make it up for tomorrow?"

Ruth patiently explains that each of them will spend the rest of the morning writing a *real* CV for the imaginary job of customer services assistant and that the CV will be sent to *real* mangers in *real* offices who they will visit for a *real* interview. It's going to be a tough two days.

First the girls have to realise that even as 13- and 14-year-olds they have something to offer. A list of possible achievements goes up on the screen: 'Have you ever made something?... Got better at something?... Passed an exam or test?... Looked after an elderly person?... Organised an event?... Cooked for someone?'

"I had to look after my six-year-old brother for a whole day when my mum was out," offers Paige. "Does that count?"

"Absolutely that counts," says Ruth, "and what quality does that demonstrate, do you think?"

"Responsibility?" suggests Paige tentatively.

Unlike Paige, some of the girls are going to find this task particularly hard. There will be some for whom the world of work is unknown, as they are familiar only with a dependency on benefits.

At exactly 10% Gorton's latest unemployment figures are above average for the whole city, which are greater than those of the NW region which, in turn, are greater than the national average. So, with Gorton near the bottom of the pile, it'd be no surprise to discover some of the girls in this room are from families who don't work and maybe, for a couple of generations at least, never have. Listening to a mother, a father, a brother or sister discuss their shift patterns, complain about their pay, or watching them iron their work clothes, bring home a colleague, or celebrate a promotion – will be unknown experiences.

"I've gotta be at work for what time? Nah! You've gotta be kidding me lady! I'm never out of bed before 12!"

For this task they have to imagine they will be the junior member in a team of six and, as well as simple admin tasks like responding to emails and answering the phone, they will have to interact with customers 'in a polite and helpful manner'. The girls take time to match their achievements, however small and insignificant they think they are, to the job description. They learn how being the captain of their sports team or sorting out an argument between friends count towards demonstrating a positive attitude or staying calm under pressure.

The girls pair off and some of them throw themselves into their alternate roles of interviewer and interviewee. "So, what can you tell me about yourself that demonstrates you are honest and reliable?"

"Look at them straight in the eye and shake their hand firmly – not too firmly! – and tell them your name. Now everyone have a go... remember the eye contact."

After lunch, and as the other Reclaim staff take turns in typing the girls' CVs, Tosin and Tasha role-play an interview where Tosin plays at first a gum-chewing, phone-toting loudmouth who sees no reason why she shouldn't immediately be offered the job and then a nail-biting, inarticulate introvert whose gaze never leaves the floor. Everyone has a huge giggle at the apparent absurdity of each situation but the Gorton Girls get the point.

The next morning, as Reclaim staff lay out Primark blouses and cardigans, Ruth takes a call from the older sister of one of the girls. She's been ill during the night, Ruth is told, and doesn't feel well enough to come today. Anticipating some refusals and after determining the 'illness' is only really a bad case of nerves, Ruth speaks to the girl and gently encourages her to come in, promising she really won't have to do the interview if she can't face it. The girl agrees and within 40 minutes she is dressed with the others in white blouse and navy cardigan.

There's a group picture before the girls and their mentors are given their instructions on where to go and who to see. The excitement and anticipation is building but before everyone heads for the appropriate bus stops there's a pep talk about first impressions and eye contact.

"We really wish we were going with you because we really care about you," says Ruth. "We know some of you are scared but what's really impressive is that everyone has come back today. So thank you for coming back, well done! And remember, keep your phones off and no chewing gum!"

As I sit at the back of the top deck with these girls, still practising their responses to the interview questions, I'm impressed at the level of interest Reclaim has managed to drum up from high-calibre local organisations. Yes, these are mock interviews and no one is walking away with the job as customer services assistant by the end of the day, but today there are a significant number of human resource professionals across the city who will be giving up their mornings to interview 13- and 14-year-old girls from Gorton. Partly this is down to the persuasive power of the Reclaim team, but mainly it is an appreciation by these organisations that they can help redress an imbalance by giving these youngsters a unique experience that will positively affect their life chances.

I first follow Tosin and her group of nervous teenagers to the offices of the British Transport Police where the HR manager immediately puts the girls at their ease by taking them all into a bright, modern

"If there's one thing you should take with you today it is this: first impressions count. Interviewers will make up their minds in the first two minutes so go in there with a big smile, look them in the eye, shake their hand and say, 'How are you?'"

boardroom to chat to them about the organisation and her role in it. She goes on to interview each in turn, smiling constantly so as not to worry the girls that their answers might not be perfect.

Then I dash across town to an unattractive, cramped 60s office block to find Paige waiting with her group in the reception area of a trade union. Since I saw her on the bus, Paige has replaced the Primark cardigan with a smart black jacket and, as she is invited into the adjacent interview room, she could easily be mistaken for a 17-year-old. After explaining myself, I slip into the interview room too. It's much smaller than the boardroom I have just left and a little more formal with two women sitting opposite Paige, one asking the pre-prepared questions, the other noting her responses.

Paige shines. She is polite, professional even, her eyes rarely leaving the faces of the two women opposite. She is enjoying this experience and looks completely relaxed. She has told me she wants to be an accountant and, listening to this confident young woman demonstrating how responsible and approachable she is, I have no doubt she will make it.

Back at the Zion the groups return one after the other, rushing to tell the staff and each other about their experiences. The girl who had been ill during the night gets a big hug as she walks in.

There's a smile on her face. "I did it," she says, visibly relieved. "I did it!"

"Listen! LISTEN!" shouts Ruth once everyone has returned. "The feedback we've had from the interviewers has been absolutely phenomenal. They said that you were amazing. You were bright, you were intelligent, you thought on your feet and you looked beautiful. Well done!"

Paige lives with her mum, Lisa, her older sister and her younger brother near the top of a dead end terraced street in Gorton. There's a primary school playing field at the end of the street which, judging by the hole in the fence, the local children use after hours.

"There's some bloke coming round," Lisa would have said to her own mother, "something about Paige and that Reclaim project. He wants to interview me. Would you come over while he's here?"

I can't be sure it was like that but, as I'm about to discover, this is a very close family who are used to supporting each other and, as I'm now sitting in front of Paige's mum *and* her nana, it's not a bad assumption to make.

It's not as if Lisa is shy. In fact she is a very confident, open woman who is more than happy to talk about her life to a complete stranger. But first her and her mother ask me more about this project that Paige is so enthusiastic about.

"At Reclaim they realise 13 to 14 is a very crucial age..." I begin.

"It is," agrees Lisa.

".... by 15 or 16 it's too late in a way. Most young people have already decided whether they are going to be bothered by then. I don't know a great deal about this myself," I have to admit, "it's just what I'm picking up."

"I was pregnant by the age of 15," says Lisa, bluntly. "Whereas Paige is just beginning to come out of herself now,

"Oh, hello Lenny. I must admit we forgot you were coming. Georgia's slept over at her mate's and Paige is still in bed. Would you like a drink? I can't have my picture taken with my hair like this, I'll have to put something on."

isn't she? For a while she couldn't be bothered but now she's just blooming."

"Tell me about that, getting pregnant at 15," I ask.

"I'd met the kids' dad when I was about 12. He used to live on the next street from us, didn't he?"

"Yeah," says Nana. "They were friends at first, just kids hanging around."

"When I got pregnant with Paige's older sister, Georgia, I didn't tell anyone for six months. I was scared of telling my parents. Me and my dad had a really close relationship and I knew he'd be devastated."

"Me and her father had been married for five years before we had Lisa," says Nana. "She was the oldest of seven and he always looked upon her as *his* little girl."

"He couldn't cope with it," recalls Lisa. "He had a nervous breakdown."

"He was frightened for her. He thought she would die in childbirth, she was so young. He was really terrified. And then, when Georgia was only eight weeks old he was killed."

"He was murdered. He got stabbed 27 times," confirms Lisa.

I'm not quite sure how to react to this horrific piece of family history. I'm intrigued to know more but I don't want to pry. "Is it okay...?"

"It's fine," says Lisa, putting me at my ease.

"Did your dad know the man who killed him?" I ask.

"Oh yeah. He was sent away for five years for manslaughter, which was disgusting. It was never manslaughter."

"So your dad never knew his grandchildren, your kids?"

"Only Georgia, very briefly. But no, he didn't, and that's very sad. He's got ten grandkids now. But my dad's death made me a strong person. I was only 15 and I'd just had Georgia and decided I had to put my whole world into her."

"And then I took with a breakdown," Nana continues, "and so she not only had an eight-week-old baby to look after but also her six younger brothers and sisters..."

"And the youngest of your siblings was how old?"

"Twenty-two months. Plus an eight-week-old. At 15," says Lisa, smiling.

"Where's Georgia's dad in all of this?"

"He was around. He was quite helpful but, at only 17, he was only a kid himself, still going out chilling with the lads and that. I just threw myself into looking after my brothers and sisters and my daughter. It's strange because it did help me get over the death of my dad. I didn't have time to think about it, I just had to get on with it."

"So you didn't have any time to grieve?"

"No, none at all. Then I got pregnant with Paige. I was 16 when we had Paige. There's just 13 months between the two girls."

"Then it got worse," says Nana.

"It was the boys," recalls Lisa referring to her younger brothers, "they went out of control. With no father figure it was very hard for them... it was a nightmare really."

"One of my sons was a world champion kick-boxer," says Nana, "and from the age of nine it had been his whole life. He went around the world competing in kick-boxing competitions. Once his dad died that was it... it didn't excite him any more because all he'd wanted to do was bring that trophy home to show his dad what he'd won."

There's mention of motorbikes, a factory roof and the police, but I'm keen to hear about the latest addition to this family in crisis.

"Tell me about Paige as a little girl: what was she like?"

"She was a beautiful little baby and an absolutely brilliant child. I don't think I would've coped if she wasn't."

"She was a good little thing, a proper good child," confirms Lisa's mum.

"When she went to primary school, they loved her from day one. I see the teachers even now, in Tesco's or wherever, and they still ask after her. She made a big impression. When me and her dad split up about two years ago she found that difficult. She started being a bit..."

"...Rebellious," finishes Nana.

"They all still see him, he's still a good dad. And Leyton, our youngest, he goes over at weekends but the girls don't because they just want to be with their mates. They chat to him on the phone to see if he's all right."

"Paige was always very close to her dad, wasn't she?" says Nana.

"It was his drinking that split us up. He had a bad drink problem and I had to put the kids first. It wasn't fair on them listening to us arguing the whole time. That's what I said to him in the end: we're better off apart."

"How is Paige now? What would you like for her..."

"I want her to finish school. I know she can do it. She's very, very clever but she's messed about and had dropped from the top sets down to group three. When her mocks came round I told her she had to put the effort in and she did. She got all As and Bs and is back in the top sets again. I didn't do any school but I want her to finish and I want her to go to college. She says she going to be an accountant. She's not interested in boys… they just hold you back, she says!"

"So it'd be a shock if she turned round to you and said…"

"Oh, do you know what? I'd be devastated! Yes, I had my girls young and it's been hard but I don't want that for them. I want them to have a nice job and a nice car and go on holiday and live their lives how they should. I'm sure they'll have babies at some point but at least they should have a life before that. No, I'd be devastated."

"We're not going to get much for £15," someone says.

"You'll be given a list of shops," says Tosin, "that I've already visited and explained to them what's going on. Tell them you're from Reclaim and they'll sell you clothes really cheaply and some said they might even have things for free."

The Reclaim team has wasted no time in organising the 'Make up your Mentor' event before the Gorton Girls graduate just before Christmas. It was hoped that this activity, based around fashion, might be more popular but as the girls, mentors, staff and volunteers gather in Reclaim's offices I can see that attendance is again disappointing.

"They thought if we suggested our own events then more would come," Alix reminds me, "but not everyone has shown up. I think it's because it's early and it's a Saturday."

Karla apparently was the first here, waiting on the pavement for the offices to be opened. I find out later that Paige hasn't shown up because last night she'd been locked out by her mother and had to spend the night at her auntie's. Others wouldn't have come because it meant bus fare into town, or going alone to an unknown venue or, as Alix suggested, it's too early (it's 10am) and Saturday is a time for chilling with friends.

As some of the Reclaim team phone round to see who else is on their way, Tosin and Ruth set out the plan for the next two days. The girls and their mentors will go shopping this morning with a £15 budget to spend in the secondhand shops around Oldham Street, come back to the office and create an outfit for a catwalk show tomorrow afternoon.

Alix has already been involved in the planning of the make-over weekend and with help from volunteers (Reclaim's friends of friends with design experience) has come up with a theme. "We've decided to base it around the seasons," Alix is now telling everyone, "and we've made up these theme boards for each season to give you some ideas for your outfits."

Within half an hour the girls and their mentors hit the shops, discovering a whole new world of 'retro' clothing that is way off their fashion radar. Yes, some shops are friendly, pulling out box after box of secondhand dresses, shoes, shawls and accessories. One woman even hands out sweets. But others are less forthcoming, only knocking a couple of pounds off their cheapest items, making the purchase of a dress for £8 one of the most expensive items of the day.

Alix is shopping with her mentor, Laura, and half-sister, Jo, who has come in a supporting role. I can see she is having a great time, bouncing ideas off the two of them. "If these two weren't with me I wouldn't have a clue," she says as I try to photograph her choosing the dress Laura will wear tomorrow.

I'd spoken to 22-year-old Laura a few weeks back about her experiences as a mentor on the Gorton Girls' project. Working full-time as a PR account handler, she couldn't make the four-day conference so first met Alix at the activity weekend in the Lake District. "She was just like a mini me!" she says, "When we first met, we were pretty much wearing the same clothes and we had our hair the same way. Everyone kept taking photos of us because they said we looked like sisters. It was really nice."

Laura says she enjoys mentoring Alix although she admits she sometimes feels out of her depth. "When we went to the cinema together she offloaded all this stuff that had been happening to her and it's very different from anything I ever experienced when I was at school. I find it hard to give advice because I just can't relate to it, but I do reassure her that it's not normal and hopefully it's some help talking it through."

After a couple of hours of bargain-hunting and bumping into each other on the pavements comparing their purchases, everyone is back at the office to prepare their outfits. There are sewing machines available and lots of advice and practical support from the volunteers. With clothes, lengths of colourful material, cheap jewelry and accessories all over

the floor, the office soon resembles the fashion and design department of a further education college. There's a buzz of industrious excitement as girls and mentors customise their outfits, sharing ideas and reels of cotton. Someone even knocks up a batman cape and mask for Emily's four-year-old son.

While burgers and subs are passed round at lunchtime I take the opportunity to put my tape recorder in front of Frances who is mentoring on her second Reclaim which, I guess, makes her something of a veteran.

"What," I ask, "do you get out of mentoring?"

"For me, the people you meet at Reclaim are all positive people, without exception. They want to be part of something special. No one is doing this for their own egos. Reclaim is a lot about giving but, in turn, you get something back. I've met some amazing new friends, people who I'd want to know for a long time."

"And what do you think is unique about the project?"

"There's a sheer passion for young people which comes from the top and is fed down to everyone who gets involved. It's infectious. It's about believing that young people deserve more opportunities and then doing something about it."

"Ten more minutes," shouts Ruth as the afternoon draws to a close but before everyone has perfected their catwalk masterpieces. "We don't want you going home in the dark. There'll be time to finish off tomorrow morning."

The next morning is even more frenetic. Not only are finishing touches being made but the make-up and hair specialists are now in full flow. Some of the girls are also getting dressed up as they will have to introduce their creations on stage. A couple of the Reclaim team are across town decorating the venue – a small nightclub friendly to the Reclaim cause – as others coordinate preparations in the office.

"Remember girls," says Tosin, "you need to write down what you are going to say. You need to prepare a script." This fun weekend might have been suggested by the girls themselves but they are not getting away lightly. Their comfort zones are going to be extended yet again when, for a couple of minutes at least, they are each centre stage.

Looking over the shoulder of one of the girls I notice she has nearly completed her introduction, '… I chose this outfit because it doesn't make her bum look too big and because it represents just what you can do with little money in shops people didn't know existed.'

Eventually everyone is ready, or as ready as they are going to be. There's much laughter as they pile out onto the street aware of the looks they are getting from passers-by. They all stick together –

"I am extremely proud of Karla for displaying her amazing creativity. A dazzling career in accessory design awaits," says Emily.

safety in numbers – as they walk the couple of hundred yards to the nightclub. Once inside they cram into the small artistes' dressing room to listen to the running order.

Although the girls have been asked to invite their families along to the show, the audience is a modest one, made up, as far as I can tell, of friends and relatives of staff and volunteers. Two girls from a previous Reclaim step up to compere the show and first they introduce two more 'graduates' who sing a beautiful acappella duet to set the scene.

Then the show begins as the girls and their mentors emerge, a pair at a time, to stand in front of the audience. Most of the girls read self-consciously from their scripts and most of the mentors pose uncomfortably in their seasonal outfits. There are exceptions and Karla is one. Only a few months previously she was a stubborn, uncooperative girl who, with arms folded, would sit and refuse to engage in any group activity. Today, this young woman stuns everyone as she clutches the microphone and, apparently without preparation, confidently declares:

"I chose this for Emily because she is quite self-conscious but I think she looks fantastic in it."

With mouths open we listen as she describes the outfit in detail with Emily, equally taken aback, making her way up and down the dance floor.

It's another defining moment on the Gorton Girls' Reclaim and one I feel honoured to have witnessed.

With the show over and Tosin's mother's rice being ladled out into plastic bowls, I get some feedback from the audience and participants. "I wasn't expecting it to be so good," says one man who I assume is a volunteer's friend or partner. "The girls were really confident with their speeches and the clothes were terrific. Really impressed all round."

I catch Alix as she passes by, two bowls of rice in hand. "How do you think Laura did?"

"Dead good. If it was me doing it I'd have been really shy but she didn't seem shy at all."

"Glad it's over?" I ask one of the mentors, the one whose bum 'didn't look too big'. "Yes!" she says.

"Where are you now? Can you walk to the library entrance on the main road and meet us there?" And then, "Okay, on the corner with Matthews Lane, we'll be there in 10 minutes."

I'm a few minutes early for the rendevous at Tesco's car park but two white limos are already waiting as are two of the Gorton Girls, Karla and Bianca.

"Keep that camera away from me," says Karla, as soon as she sees me. I interpret this as a greeting as my camera isn't yet out of my bag.

It's bitterly cold and both girls are shivering as they stand on the corner next to the limos, maybe hoping that someone they know will pass by and they can confirm that, yes, these cars are taking them into town for their graduation ceremony.

"I'm starving," Karla says to Bianca.

"Me, too."

Turns out that neither of them has eaten so far today although it is after two in the afternoon. "If I give you a couple of quid each will you get something from Tesco while we're waiting?" I ask. The girls don't need much encouragement and run off towards the store entrance.

Tosin and Jess from the Reclaim team arrive and tick off names as more girls congregate, few of them dressed for the freezing temperatures. "My nose is about to fall off," I hear one woman declare to her partner as they head for the warmth of the supermarket.

With 20 names on the list there's a momentary worry there won't be enough space in the limos for all the girls and the adults accompanying them. But, fifteen minutes after the scheduled meeting time, we are still short of five girls who, a few days ago, had confirmed they would definitely be attending.

Karla and Bianca are back. They have a multipack of muffins from the supermarket and a cone of chips each from Savori's café in the indoor market across the way. As the girls take shelter in the limos – the chip-eaters have to finish their breakfast first – Tosin and Jess begin to phone round trying to track down the missing girls. Some are ready and willing to come but live too far from the meeting point to walk on the icy pavements and so we make arrangements to pick them up on the way. Tosin tells me later that a few couldn't come because, although they wanted to, their parents wouldn't bring them (apparently one father refused to get out of bed) or wouldn't let them travel alone, as the girls would have to make their own way home after the graduation.

As we are waiting I ask a few of the girls whether their families are coming along later to watch them graduate. Reclaim has negotiated the free use of one entire floor of a new, but as yet still empty, office block in a recently-completed development near Piccadilly. All the parents and carers have this week received invitations and directions to the venue. Everyone and anyone is invited, there's no restriction on places. But as I ask around it's clear that more than half the girls will only be sharing this special occasion with the Reclaim team, their mentors and the other girls. This saddens me and yet reinforces the challenging backdrops against which many of the Gorton Girls play out their young lives.

"Okay, let's go," says Tosin, "if we wait any longer, we'll be late."

Up on the seventh floor of the high-tech office block friends and families gather as dusk falls across a panoramic cityscape. Thankfully there's a reasonable crowd despite significant parental absences. Mentors, volunteers and Reclaim friends swell the numbers. Alix's family are here and Paige, as expected, has plenty of support. Karla's nana is sitting towards the back with Karla's sisters, Michaela,

Loretta and Sonya, a recent mum who's brought both her fiancé and eight-week old daughter, asleep and tiny. I'm delighted Karla's mother is here too, which I wasn't expecting.

The Gorton Girls, way on the other side and out of sight, pull black graduation gowns off a clothes rail as if they're searching for sale bargains. There's banter as they get ready:

"Is this the only colour they've got?" says one girl. "If you have to wear one of these at uni or wherever, then I'm not going," says someone else.

Teenage hair-dos and mortar boards are incompatible and for a few of the girls this fashion disaster gets in the way of this significant occasion. "Just put them on as you walk in," suggests Ruth, "after that just hold them on your knees."

Paige is in her element. She looks as if this might be the real thing and is one of the first to stride to the 'stage' and take her place in the front row. The others follow: 15 young women ill-at-ease in their gowns and even more uncomfortable now as the centre of attention at their own Reclaim graduation. Fifteen out of the 20 who should have been here today and out of 28 who started on the first day of the conference all those months ago.

With all the girls settled, Ruth kicks off the informal proceedings with an introduction about what these young women have achieved since April:

"You are all so bright and capable,"

she tells them; and why this event is so important to them:

"We're hoping that some of you are going to be wearing these 'silly' hats for your real graduation days before long.

The Gorton Girls

"Don't let people tell you that where you're from means you're not going to achieve. There are lots of fantastic jobs in Manchester and you girls, in a few years time, need to be getting those jobs. Are you listening?"

Before certificate scrolls are presented there are other short talks and accolades. Karla comes forward with her mentor, Emily, who tells everyone how they got to know each other during the conference and how she, Emily, was so pleased to be paired with Karla. "I can't wait to see how she develops and what she achieves because she knows deep down inside she will do great things. She's got that strength inside to do well and I'm really proud of her and so glad to have met her."

Each of the Gorton Girls is called forward to receive their scrolls and I do my best to capture the individual presentations although the girls are eager to retreat from the spotlight as quickly as possible.

Next, members of the Reclaim team present special awards, each reading a citation and building up the suspense. The winner of the positivity award is, "... a bright young woman who has impressed everyone by her energy and enthusiasm. She always goes the extra mile to achieve all she can in challenges and tasks. Her bubbly personality is pleasant to be around and she continues to maintain a positive outlook and attitude." Of course, it can only be Alix who steps up to collect this award, the young woman who has always been focussed and enthusiastic in everything I have documented over these last months.

After Latisha collects her award for confidence and bravery and Bianca picks up one for dedication, Ruth begins to read the script for the final award, for outstanding contribution. "It's an overall award," she reads, "for a young person who has excelled in every area."

Karla has yet to receive a special award and I'm quietly hopeful she gets this last one. Hers was the first family I visited, the first story I heard. She hasn't been the most attentive nor cooperative of the

Gorton Girls but she's put so much of herself into Reclaim and, well, I listen now with anticipation to the final citation.

"This award," continues Ruth, "goes to a young woman who has grown with every challenge. She has given as much as she has gained from Reclaim. She started the project really lacking in confidence," – it must be Karla – "and has developed into a funny and sparkling, beautiful young woman who makes us laugh and impresses us all with her tireless dedication. She has never missed a Reclaim event," – definitely Karla – "and has produced some stunning work over the previous eight months. She has a huge heart and has been supportive of the project, her family and her mentor. She is not yet aware of just how special she is to us all and we look forward to seeing her have a bright, really positive, wonderful Gorton future. The person who has won the outstanding contribution award is... Karla."

There are whoops and cheers from the audience as Karla again comes forward. Ruth's hug knocks her mortar board backwards as I step up to record the moment. Karla is stunned, embarrassed and truly delighted. Maybe it's the first time she has experienced anything like this. Her grandad would be proud.

"These amazing young people would come to the end of our life-changing project brimming with confidence and raring to go, so it was naive to think we would just wish them luck and wave goodbye. They wanted more and we needed to give them more."

Ruth Ibegbuna

RECLAIM:ED

The aim of the graduate programme is to further develop the skills the young people have learnt on the Reclaim project. The graduates are given the opportunity to link up with local businesses, work independently and find out more about the world of work. They are then trained to lead their own workshops and events in their own communities.

"It's a two-stage programme. The first stage, up until the age of 16, is to offer them training sessions with businesses supervised by a professional mentor. They might, for example, do a weekly placement after school in a local business, working towards personalised goals.

"The next stage is for them to become peer mentors and champions for certain projects. They'd be offered training opportunities – leading to qualifications – after which they could lead their own workshops and events. Remember, the criteria for choosing particular young people for a Reclaim project in the first place is for their leadership potential and Reclaim:ed should bring that full circle. We want young people to have the confidence, skill and expertise to give back something to their neighbourhoods."

Abi Robertson, Reclaim:ed graduate programme coordinator

Abi: The Co-operative Gym Project gave us the inspiration for our graduate programme. It came about through a happy coincidence of events.

Ruth: I'd spoken at a business event at the Hilton where I was the fluffy feel-good after dinner speech. I finished with a call to action and asked anyone who might be interested to get in touch. Kate Morris from The Co-operative Group called me.

Abi: Eight girls from the South Manchester Girls' Reclaim came to see us at the beginning of the summer holidays in 2009 and asked for something to do. At the same time The Co-operative was keen to help support Reclaim and so we were able to put the two together on a project to design the gym for their new head office.

Kate Morris, head of corporate estates and services at The Co-operative: I was particularly keen to support women in business and

this was an opportunity to get involved at grass roots level and work with young people who wouldn't normally get this chance. For the entire six weeks of the holidays the girls worked with us and our design team, 3DReid, on the design of our new gym.

Abi: The young women had developed skills from Reclaim that they were able to put into practice on this 'live' project. The eight girls chosen show particular potential for leadership in business.

They were given a budget for their expenses and had to account for all their comings and goings; they undertook research; had weekly

Reclaim:ed – the graduate programme

feedback sessions with The Co-operative and, at the end of the project, made a formal presentation to the mayor and staff from The Co-operative and Reclaim.

Alieh, project participant: Getting feedback from the Co-op was a highlight for me. It made you feel good that you'd done something right.

Jaimeel, project participant: I was involved in the research and so I went to lots of different gyms around the city, found out how they were run and how much the equipment cost. It taught me how to organise myself and how to work with other people.

Tyler, project participant: The best bit for me was working with 3DReid... I want to be an architect.

Kate: They learnt about teamwork, target setting, design processes, keeping their target audience in mind. All the principles they developed, all their design ideas, will be reflected in the new gym.

Jahlica, project participant: I've learnt that anything is possible if you put your mind to it.

Kate: It'd be great to invite the girls back once the gym is complete in a couple of years from now. They could see how their work has been put into practice and we could see how they have developed.

Ruth: Doing The Co-operative Gym Project made us realise there are possibilities within the private sector that are much more straightforward. If we fit their objectives then things can happen very quickly.

Peter is a manager in the Estates Department of The Co-operative Group. Jahlica is a 16-year-old schoolgirl from Gorton in east Manchester.

They first met when she and her Reclaim friends helped design the gym for The Co-operative's new head office, (see previous pages). Now she is giving her input into design ideas for the 'public realm', the open spaces around the head office building.

Jahlica: "Before, I was quite quiet and shy; I never wanted to get involved in anything like this. This has boosted my confidence loads. I'd never have been able to come and have a conversation with a business person... now I'm eager to get involved with everything."

Peter: "For me, it's about going out of my way to include Jahlica positively. Having her on the team will bring real benefits — there's nothing tokenistic about her involvement. I enjoy helping people and I get so much, personally and professionally, from this relationship.

"I love the whole idea of Reclaim and find it inspiring to be working with such a receptive individual as Jahlica."

During the summer of 2010 eight Reclaim graduates were recruited to work as 'city hosts' in Manchester's city centre.

After completing an intensive training programme they spent six weeks acting as ambassadors for the city offering information about events and attractions and giving advice to visitors.

The initiative, managed by Cityco, the city centre management company, gave some young people their first experience of paid employment.

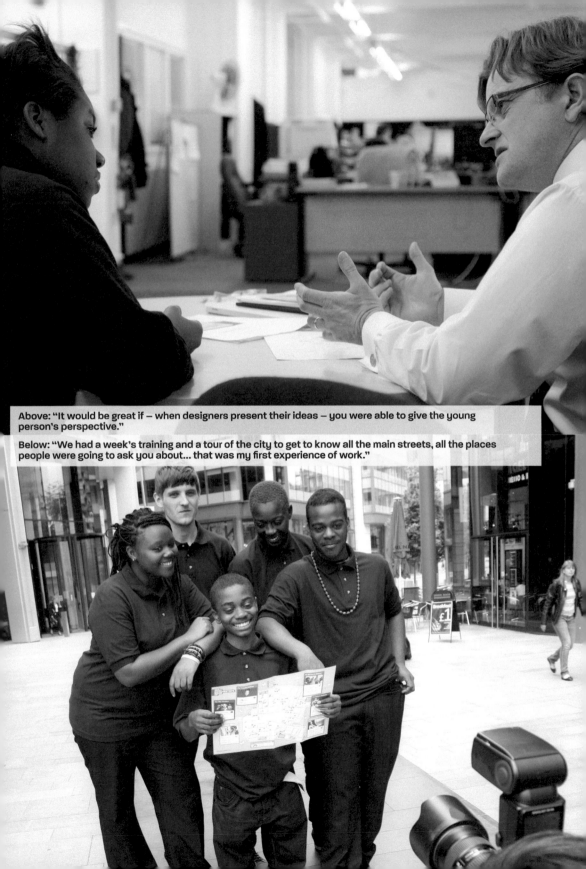

Above: "It would be great if — when designers present their ideas — you were able to give the young person's perspective."

Below: "We had a week's training and a tour of the city to get to know all the main streets, all the places people were going to ask you about... that was my first experience of work."

At a breakfast meeting to encourage more businesses onto the Reclaim:ed programme: "We want to ground Reclaim in giving these young people real life chances. They need be made aware of what opportunities are out there."

Bonnie's story is a little unusual. The Reclaim team visited her school in Blackley and subsequently chose some participants for a North Manchester Girls' project. Bonnie wasn't one of them. Undeterred, she turned up at Reclaim's city centre offices one day after school and practically demanded to be let on the project. She wasn't refused.

Following her graduation, Bonnie took up a placement on Reclaim:ed, the developing programme for Reclaim graduates.

Her work experience at the Heritage Lottery Fund's North West Regional offices will run for at least twelve months.

"I wouldn't say I was overly confident before Reclaim but then I wasn't really shy either. I was somewhere in the middle and I think people in the middle don't get as much attention because we haven't got any problems – or it doesn't seem that way – and you don't get noticed if you haven't got any problems. You get forgotten about. That's when I started not to care.

"My Reclaim project was life-changing. It changed me and my opinion of things."

"Now I'm noticed and that's something new. I feel better as a person because I'm recognised as having a positive attitude.

"For the last six weeks I've been researching the idea of a Facebook page for the HLF's North West Region and now I'm working on a presentation I'm making to senior managers in a couple of weeks.

"A Facebook page would help young people get more involved in the organisation. They'd find it easier to get the information that way. I already know a lot about Facebook but I have been looking at other HLF regions' pages and thinking how we could do it differently.

"In school if we're working on a project then it wouldn't be for something real. This is a real project, it's not pretend. It's worthwhile and creative and it makes me feel grown-up."

Iain Kinnear, development officer at the HLF, says:

"It's impressive that someone of Bonnie's age will make the time to come to our offices after school and work with us for a couple of hours each week. She is extremely motivated and engaged and has become a valuable member of the team, impressing us all with her insightful comments in important meetings.

"I remember my own work placement was very much about making the tea and doing bits of photocopying. It certainly didn't give you any passion or inspiration for a career. Nowadays employers don't think of university as the pinnacle of achievement but getting into the workplace early is just as relevant.

"The Reclaim:ed programme is really quite innovative in its introduction to work. It's designed with the young person at the centre and I've been particularly impressed with Reclaim's expectation from employers. It's very much a two-way process and I know I have to invest my time to make it worthwhile. That's what's made it distinctive: the professionalism and the ambition."

"Reclaim affects the young people in different ways.
For some it's a significant lifestyle choice.
They're 'On Reclaim' and this means something
serious about the way they live their lives.
They can be evangelical about it, telling parents,
teachers and friends and working hard to spread
the word beyond those in the know.

"For others, the graduation day is their last
Reclaim experience: they've enjoyed the
project, have good memories, but now it's
finished... and that's okay too. For many, they
only realise what Reclaim is trying to do after
they have graduated or perhaps when life
gets tough and they get back in touch and
we're still there for them."

Ruth Ibegbuna

Where Are They Now?

Terry's on track now but it hasn't been easy. He successfully completed the first ever Reclaim project but a 'crazy moment' at school set him back.

I really enjoyed Reclaim, it was like getting ready for the world. Doing the job interviews really helped. We got tips and advice and useful feedback, it was definitely one of my highlights. That and going down to London to meet an MP and having a tour round the capital.

It was during Reclaim that I got much more politically aware. I'd always been interested in politics but I remember picking up some BNP literature and getting mad with the way they were promoting themselves. Their leaflets were written very simply, without being openly racist, and I'm sure voters didn't really understand what the BNP stood for.

I started writing letters to the other parties, encouraging them to make their manifestos more easily understood, especially by young people. There was no way people my age were going to be interested in politics if they couldn't understand what the parties were telling them. I produced my own newsletter about politics and had it printed and distributed and that experience was really good. It encouraged me and made me realise I wanted to be a journalist.

Terry:
"At that time voters were becoming fed up with mainstream politicians and the BNP were gaining support from people who wouldn't normally vote for them."

At that time I was doing well at school. I didn't have a record of bad behaviour and yet I lost the plot for one stupid moment and paid the price. I was kicked out of school and I don't blame anyone for that but me. But Reclaim didn't disown me. In fact, I'd be in a lot more trouble if it wasn't for them. Whilst I was excluded I'd go down to their offices and work there. They were constantly supportive.

Terry eventually moved to another school and is now at a sixth-form college studying English, sports and IT. He writes for the college newspaper, continues to be politically active and is about to start a blog.

Najee was 13 when he was recruited onto the Moss Side Boys' Reclaim in 2007.

The youngest of four, he was born in Jamaica but moved to England when he was five, after his parents split up. Moss Side has been his home since then. Now 17, he is studying media at college and plans to go onto university and become a teacher.

Actually my brothers have all got that leadership thing about them, especially my big brother. He's been a massive influence. I've always had it, but Reclaim brought it out much more.

I'd have younger kids calling round, asking for me, asking for advice. And there was this one time — exam time — when my teacher came to my house to talk to me and my mum. He asked if I would talk to these two in my year who hadn't completed their coursework. He knew I had a positive influence. So I did speak to them and they did finish their coursework. My mum couldn't believe it.

During my Reclaim I was the one who did most of the talking. They were always saying, 'Let Najee do the talking,' and I didn't mind. I will talk to anyone, it's just talking isn't it? But I did get a bit nervous when we went down to the Houses of Parliament and I had to talk to them. But yeah, it was Reclaim who showed me I had leadership skills; they triggered it off.

Since the project, me and my friends have started our own mentoring programme. We've called ourselves 'Goodfellows' and we're only just getting going. We've been on the local community radio and working with an adult mentor because sometimes you need an adult to push things forward.

Najee: "We're going to start a new type of youth club when we're older. Young people will come because they want to, but they'll have to focus.

We've launched this campaign called Nii which stands for 'Not In It'. We've had t-shirts printed with Nii across the front and they're to be worn with pride by anyone who wants to stay focussed.

When I turn 18 me and four friends are going to open a youth club. But it won't be like an ordinary youth club, with football and that, it'll be run by the people themselves and it'll be a bit like school but not compulsory.

Sacha: All the girls on our Reclaim were picked for different reasons. Some because they had anger issues, some because they were shy; it depended on the person...

Latoya: It could have been because they lacked confidence or had problems at home. We don't actually know why we were nominated. I know for Sacha it was because of her confidence and things that had gone on in her life and it was the same for me – confidence and stuff that had happened at home.

S: We'd be different people if we hadn't done Reclaim. I don't know what I'd do without Reclaim, it's changed us so much.

L: Reclaim has really given me confidence. Before, if you'd ask me to stand on a stage in front of a whole crowd of people and give a speech...

S: ... and make it up as you go along...

L: ... then I'd have run off screaming. But that's exactly what I've done since Reclaim. My confidence has really been built up, but then more things have happened and it dropped back down a bit...

S: ... but it's going back up. It's getting there.

Sacha, left, and Latoya: "The best bit? There wasn't one best bit, there were loads. We loved it... and still do."

Latoya has been at the heart of Reclaim since she attended the South Manchester Girls' project. She is relentlessly optimistic and refuses to accept any form of social inequality. This has led to some rather fiery dialogue with the local and national politicians she meets on Reclaim's behalf when she feels they are not being sincere.

In 2010 Sacha won Manchester City Council's Young Woman of the Year Award for her volunteering work with Reclaim and for demonstrating remarkable courage in overcoming difficult personal circumstances. She is the young person's representative on the Reclaim board of trustees.

Jordan is one of seven siblings. He lives in Bolton with his father and younger sister.

I couldn't control my anger and it was getting worse. At school I had a reputation for kicking off and I felt good about that. Some little kid told me once that he wanted to be like me. But one day I went too far and attacked a teacher which got me excluded.

I wasn't sure about Reclaim at first. I nearly didn't go on the first day. But everyone was sound, everyone was normal. I remember the manifesto day perfectly. I'd written, 'Give young people a chance,' and 'Take pride in where you come from'. To be honest, when we were giving them out I don't think people took us very seriously.

Jordan became a valued participant on the Bolton Boys' Reclaim, throwing himself into all the activities with enthusiasm and building a new reputation as the group's spokesman. He represented Reclaim on visits to politicians – even reducing one to tears – and spoke about the project at community meetings. He was amongst the boys who handed an anti-racism petition to his local mayor. Jordan changed completely during Reclaim.

Before I came on the project I was an idiot always messing about in school, and I didn't care about my education. I didn't care what happened in my life, didn't have any confidence and hated talking in front of large groups. I was a racist and all I cared about was myself and that got me nowhere.

Now I've got the confidence to do things I never thought I could and I'm trying everything I can to get back on track with my studying. My behaviour has improved and now I'm not bothered about being the tough guy, I've got my life back and I thank Reclaim for that.

At his graduation ceremony Jordan spoke about how the Reclaim project had changed him and how his dad had supported him. Later he and another Reclaim graduate organised a football fun day in support of Bolton Hospice that raised nearly £300. After some months in a pupil referral unit, Jordan moved to a new secondary school where he is catching up on seven months' school work.

At his graduation Jordan was presented with an 'ambassador's award' for his commitment to the Bolton Boys' project.

Frances lives in Moss Side and was on the first girls' project. Despite setbacks since she graduated she still feels 'reclaimed'. Between her mother and her father she has four brothers and seven sisters. She lives with her mother and one of her older brothers.

Even when I was younger, I never wanted to be at home. I felt like me and my mum were nothing and I didn't want to be in the house just in case we had an argument, so I'd stay out really, really late. When I was about nine I couldn't cope at home and ended up putting myself in care for a while because of my mum and her drinking. All I really wanted was to go to school and be a normal little girl.

I can't remember why I was chosen for Reclaim. I thought it was for people who came from really rubbish backgrounds that needed a boost. And I needed a boost then. I was in Year 8 and wasn't really getting on well with my mum, or my brother and I felt really low because of it. Me and my brother wouldn't talk, we'd just argue or he'd bully me. I had no one to talk to, or to tell any of my problems to. I was coming home from school, cooking, cleaning, basically doing the mum role and having a really, really bad day. I'd go to sleep late, then wouldn't go to school the next day. Sometimes I wouldn't go to school for months and months and my mum kept getting fines because my attendance wasn't good.

I didn't have any confidence or motivation so I thought I'd give Reclaim a go. The other girls were different to me – thinking about what they were going to wear the next day – but I wasn't like that at all. I was more excited about what Reclaim was going to teach me. I just wanted to be focussed so I never really got on well with them.

I remember one time we went out handing out manifestos in Chorlton and you had to be really confident to stand there and say 'Please read our manifesto'. Even when I got home I was going round my area and handing them out because I felt so proud of being part of Reclaim.

One of my favourites was the mock interview. It was in town somewhere – I can't remember where – but it was really good. Afterwards they told us what needed improvement and all they said for me it was my eye contact. So, since then, every time I speak to someone I have lots of eye contact.

When things started to change for me on Reclaim I wanted my home life to change immediately. I felt everything was going to get better because I felt differently. I had lots of ideas, I'd made up rules we could have in the house to make things better. We'd share out the cleaning, things like that. But it didn't really happen. My mum wasn't bothered. At the time I felt like my mum wasn't bothered about anything I did really.

And so after Reclaim, when nothing else in my life changed, it all went a bit downhill. I went 'proper teenager' doing crazy and outrageous things, staying out dead late at night again, chilling with the wrong people, with older guys, and just getting into so much trouble. I felt I had nothing and I was just living for the moment. It was rubbish. But something really bad happened and I ended up having to stop. Then I came out of that life and started becoming a bit more normal again.

I'm doing my GCSEs this year but I don't really like school. I know everyone probably says this but the teachers don't understand me or help me. We had a revision class for maths the other day and I felt like all they were doing was concentrating on the smart kids. It's as if they've given up on us already.

I did want to be a vet because I love animals but that's really competitive so now I want to go to college and do a beauty therapy level 2 course.

Reclaim was good for me, I got more confidence and I started growing up. Me and my brother have a bit more family connection going on now. We talk to each other more and don't really argue. Me and my mum are fine. She does most of the cooking. I do the cleaning sometimes.

"It's like a community, a family. They encourage you all the time to do stuff that you never thought you'd be able to do.

"If it wasn't for Reclaim I would have just gone to school, maybe gone to college and just ended up normal. Now I've had all those opportunities I'm normal, but with a twist."

Jaimeel

"I was 12 when I was picked for Reclaim and I first sang during the rapping activity at the conference. Since then everyone knew I was a singer. Then I sang at the graduation and after that I was given loads of singing opportunities. I've sung at the Palace Hotel, the Britannia Hotel, I've even sung in front of Prince Charles at Gorton Monastery. Singing in front of royalty, it felt like I'd achieved something. It felt good."

Alieh

After years of horrific domestic abuse and a series of traumatic personal crises, Elvis's mother eventually found refuge with her four children in Gorton, Manchester. Originally from Sierra Leone she is awaiting refugee status and her family continue to receive asylum seeker allowance.

My childhood was rough. We were home-schooled, we never stepped out of that house. My father was alcoholic and he'd often beat my mum. There was one time when he was going at her with a knife and I stepped in and was badly cut... it's hard to talk about.

I'm so happy I got entered to do Reclaim.

I enjoyed working with my mentor, Matt. He was the most helpful guy ever. From the minute we met on the first day he started helping me. I felt very comfortable talking to him; he just built up my courage the whole time.

I've definitely changed through Reclaim. I now feel like a leader. I feel more responsible, supporting my mum. While I was on Reclaim we had to move to Wigan. We'd never even heard of Wigan. I had to travel back to Manchester for the Reclaim activities and I know my mum found it hard with the fares, but Reclaim helped. They helped too with groceries in those first weeks because my mum's Home Office allowance hadn't come through and we had nothing. I don't know what we would have done without the shopping that Reclaim bought for us.

At first no one spoke to me at my new school. They knew I was from Manchester and they thought I was a bad boy because they thought Manchester was a dangerous place. But I reassured them and they got to know me and now I've got some new mates.

I play up front for Garswood FC, Under 15s. We're seventh in our league. I'd like to be a professional footballer but I know I need to get good grades in case that doesn't work out.

Reclaim has helped me so much... and helped my family too. My mum has had someone to talk to, to help solve her problems. They have been so supportive.

Elvis:
"Going down to London to meet Lenny Henry was the best. I'd never been to London before, I'd never worn a suit before. I spoke to him and collected an award from him. He is something else: the sort of guy you can look up to."

Although I could achieve at school I could also easily get distracted from my work by others around me. Then I'd go in a strop whenever I got told off. My teacher said Reclaim could help me with that. So I got nominated to help me keep on track.

I didn't want to go at first because I'd heard rumours that Reclaim was only for the 'brat' kids, the under-achievers. Then I thought I'd just go for the first day and see how it went.

Living in Moss Side I've joined many projects in the past which have only lasted for a week or so. The first day has been great and then nobody turns up, including the staff, and things start getting cancelled and forgotten about. So I went on that first day not expecting much and now, three years later, I'm still involved with the project. They said it wasn't going to be short-term and it hasn't been.

Reclaim has changed me. By the end of the project I didn't get angry any more and I was much more focussed, and that was down to Reclaim. When I heard people slag off my area I always wanted to say something back but I never had the courage. Now I do. Reclaim has given me a voice and I can speak my mind.

Our mentors were very important to us. They contacted us every day to see if we were okay: my mentor called, texted, emailed or Facebooked me every single day for at least the first six months. If we had a problem, they'd help to find a solution. It's like having a friend, someone you can trust. I think it's been the contact from our mentors which has kept many of us on track.

If I hadn't done Reclaim then I wouldn't be involved in all the community work I do now. They gave me a head start. I'm a volunteer with other groups in my area: I help with events, with carnival and I help other young people with their projects too. People in my area know me now as a community leader. They know me on Facebook too: the first group I made – the 'Stop The Gun Crime' group – had 2000 followers within four days. I've never been tempted with gangs myself. I know people who are in gangs and I've been offered to go in gangs but I've always wanted to stop gangs rather than be part of them.

Akeim:
"People always think my area must be a really rough place but it's just the media that make it out like that. I try and prove to them that all those stereotypes are untrue."

With Reclaim you've always got support. At the beginning it was Ruth who we knew but then Laura came on board too. When Ruth wasn't there, Laura was there. When Ruth wasn't available, then Laura was available. If there were any problems it was Ruth and Laura who came to see us. On weekends, if we needed help with our homework, it was Laura we were calling. If we called at one in the morning – and I have done – they were always there. If it wasn't for them, we wouldn't be who we are today. They stayed on track and did what they had to do, and we rate them for that.

In 2009 Akeim won the Young Achiever of the Year Award sponsored by the Jamaican Society. The following year he won another young achiever award, this time from a local community group. He is now studying for a BTEC National Diploma in Health and Social Care at Trafford College. He lives in Moss Side with his parents and older brother.

Ebony is on line for straight As and A*s in her upcoming GCSEs. She has been invited to apply for a scholarship at a south Manchester private school and is hoping to study 3D design, art, history and physics at A-level.

I've always been interested in art but since the Co-op project (see page 112) I've become much more interested in architecture. After working on that I went on a couple of CABE [Commission for Architecture and the Built Environment] projects which I really enjoyed. One was in Manchester where we had to look at a couple of old office blocks in the city centre and decide what should replace them once they got knocked down. With the help from some architects our group designed a youth centre, making models and working on the computer. We presented our ideas at Liverpool Cathedral which was good. Before I started Reclaim I was really shy and wouldn't talk to anyone. I would never have been able to get up on a stage and speak out, but at the Cathedral I felt confident and wasn't nervous at all.

A Reclaim Timeline

Dec 2005 Ruth pitches Reclaim idea in her interview for Director of Learning and Community at Urbis, Manchester's centre of urban culture.

Sept 2006 15-year-old Jesse James murdered by unknown assailants in Moss Side.

June 2007 Reclaim proposal sent to the Moss Side community, shops, schools, city councillors for consultation and feedback.

July 2007 Positive responses received from the community.

July 2007 Laura Pottinger starts volunteering on the project. She works alongside Ruth for three years on all aspects of Reclaim.

Sept 2007 Following funding shortfall, 27 mentors come forward from the community and offer to mentor for free.

Sept 2007 Forty-five 12- and 13-year-old boys nominated from seven schools.

Sept 2007 Reclaim branding conceived by Urbis intern, Sana.

Oct 2007 Moss Side Boys' project starts at Urbis with support from Odd Theatre Company.

Mar 2008 Ruth wins Manchester Evening News Peace Activist of the Year Award.

June 2008 South Manchester Girls' project begins.

July 2008 Moss Side Boys' graduation.

Aug 2008 The Silenced Majority by Eric Allison appears in The Guardian responding to issues around media representation raised by the Moss Side Boys.

Sept 2008 Moss Side Boys win National Crimebeat Awards.

Sept 2008 Home Secretary, Jacqui Smith MP, Communities Secretary, Hazel Blears MP and Arlene McCarthy MEP meet South Manchester Girls during the Labour Party Conference in Manchester.

Sept 2008 South Manchester Girls make the cover of the Times Educational Supplement.

Oct 2008 Black Panther Emory Douglas and the Art of Revolution exhibition launches at Urbis. Emory leads a masterclass in art, politics and culture with Reclaim young people.

Oct 2008 Chris Huhne MP meets with a group of Moss Side young people to encourage them to engage politically.

Nov 2008 Ruth and Laura decide to expand the project into different communities and areas.

Dec 2008 Funding shortfall curtails South Manchester Girls' project.

Dec 2008 Reclaim wins the Philip Lawrence Award.

Feb 2009 South Manchester Girls' graduation.

Feb 2009 Gorton Boys' 2009 project begins.

Apr 2009 Gorton Boys' activism weekend – Gerald Kaufman MP visits and endorses the work of the project.

May 2009 Reclaim team expands: Abi, Emma and Melissa join Ruth and Laura.

May 2009 Submit bid to central government for Inspiring Communities Grant Programme for Gorton, based on Gorton Boys' ideas.

June 2009 Reclaim visits Westminster to meet James Brokenshire MP (Conservative); David Blunkett MP(Labour) and Chris Huhne MP (Liberal Democrat).

July 2009 Graduates, Matthew and Issac, are keynote speakers at the ACPO National Policing Conference in Manchester.

July 2009 Terry, a Moss Side Boys' graduate, is disturbed to read Nick Griffin's comments on British immigration. He writes a letter to all the political parties, including the BNP, so his voice is heard. See page 122.

July-Sept 2009 Eight graduates from the South Manchester Girls' project work with senior managers and top architects on The Co-operative gym project. See page 112.

Aug 2009 Channel 4's Dispatches features Reclaim as a model case study.

Aug 2009 Reclaim wins £450,000 from the Inspiring Communities Grant Programme for the Gorton area. Gorton People Stronger Together is subsequently set up.

Sept 2009 Gorton Boys' 2009 graduation.

Oct 2009 Reclaim Boys are featured as the cover story of the Guardian's Weekend magazine.

Oct 2009 North Manchester Girls' project beings. Kemi and Tasha Ryan (see page 36); Emily Powell (page 50) and Helen Newlove are keynote speakers.

Nov 2009 Bolton Boys' project begins.

Nov 2009 Announcement that Urbis will close and re-open in 2011 as the National Football Museum. Most staff face redundancy.

Nov 2009 Reclaim hear that one of the team will be made redundant.

Dec 2009 Reclaim wins Plain English Award for manifestos.

Jan 2010 Offshoot Northern Stars project begins. Seven girls from the North Manchester project raise money for orphaned children in West Africa.

Jan 2010 Offshoot hip hop project begins and singing group, Re:verb, is formed as a result.

Jan 2010 Bolton Boys create positive artwork for Bolton train station which generates lots of press coverage.

Feb 2010 Over 70% of Urbis staff are made redundant. All Reclaim staff retained.

Feb 2010 Inspiring Communities consultation day. Over 700 Gorton residents engage in positive dialogue with Reclaim young people about the needs of their area.

Mar 2010 As part of the Bolton Boys' project, Jordan Jones, 14, speaks at a neighbourhood meeting about how Reclaim has helped him. See page 125.

Mar 2010 Moss Side graduate, Akeim, 16, appeals to the Manchester business community for new office space for Reclaim.

Apr 2010 Gorton Girls' project begins.

Apr 2010 Re:verb sing on Tim Westwood's 1Xtra Radio Show.

June 2010 Laura leaves and Jess joins the Reclaim team.

June 2010 Bolton Boys' graduation.

July 2010 Reclaim graduates quiz Ed Miliband MP during his Labour Party leadership campaign.

July 2010 New structure for the National Football Museum is unveiled. Reclaim is no longer part of core provision and redundancies for whole team are confirmed.

Aug 2010 North Manchester Girls' graduation.

Aug 2010 Reclaim staff leave Urbis.

Sept 2010 Reclaim sets up as an independent company seeking charitable status. Office space is provided by Bruntwood and funding by the Paul Hamlyn Foundation.

Sept 2010 South Manchester Girls' graduate, Sacha, wins Manchester City Council's Young Woman of the Year Award. See page 124.

Sept 2010 Re:verb sing for HRH Prince Charles at Gorton Monastery.

Oct 2010 North Manchester Boys' project begins.

Oct 2010 Bolton graduates raise money for Bolton Hospice. See page 125.

Oct 2010 North Manchester Girls' graduate, Bonnie, meets Manchester's Lord Mayor and Lady Mayoress to seek advice about improving her neighbourhood.

Nov 2010 Gorton Boys' 2010 project begins.

Nov 2010 Bolton Mentors win Vinspired – The National Young Volunteers Service – Connect Award.

Dec 2010 Reclaim:ed graduate programme breakfast launch with Manchester's business community. See page116.

Dec 2010 Re:verb put on a Christmas concert in Manchester's Piccadilly Gardens. See page 128.

Jan 2011 Reclaim achieves registered charity status.

Reclaim thanks Bruntwood, Phil Buckle, Cisco, the Paul Hamlyn Foundation and Urbis for their generosity and support. Thanks guys!

Reclaim is an independent registered charity no. 1139807

About the author

My dad works in the attic as a freelance photographer and writer. He started snapping before I was born, mostly hanging around on building sites. For the past few years he has practically lived in east Manchester, documenting the effects of urban regeneration on people's lives. In 2010 he published a rather good book called Billy and Rolonde about individual stories of social exclusion. *Rebecca, 16.*

www.lengrant.co.uk.

Published in 2011 by Len Grant Photography on behalf of those nice people at
Reclaim Project
Suite 3B2, Portland Buildings
Portland Street
Manchester M1 4PZ
www.reclaimproject.org.uk

ISBN: 978-0-9526720-8-1
Distributed by Cornerhouse, Manchester (www.cornerhouse.org/books).

Designed by Alan Ward at Axis (www.axisgraphicdesign.co.uk).
A catalogue record of this book is available from the British Library if you're passing.